COLLEGE FAQ BOOK

Over 5,000 *NOT* Frequently Asked Questions About College

Rozalia Williams, Ed.D.

College FAQ Book.
Library of Congress Control Number: 2004095499
ISBN 0975510304
First printing.

Single copies of this book may be ordered, prepaid from:
Hidden Curriculum Education, Inc., P.O. Box 222041,
Hollywood, FL 33022.
Quantity discounts are available on bulk purchases for educational or gift purposes. Visit *www.collegefaqbook.com* for more information.

Edited by Christine Belleris and Joseph Zolner
Cover design by Andrea Perrine Brower and Liliana Gonzalez
Inside book design by Dawn Von Strolley Grove
Production coordinated by Sandy Dolan

This book is dedicated to my parents
Raphu and Charlotte Williams
who taught me to ask questions;
and to my children, Satonya, Marshall,
Myron and Marcellus,
who grew up answering my questions.

Contents

Part I:
FAQs About Getting into College

Part II:
FAQs About Staying in College

PART III:
FAQs ABOUT GETTING OUT OF COLLEGE

Acknowledgments

Looking back as I move forward, I thank Carl Williams, my high school counselor for helping me get in college; Roy I. Mitchell and Corrine Brown, my college mentor and counselor, for shepherding me through my first year; Steve C. McArthur for preparing me for my first real job in higher education; Betty Bigby Young for hiring me, and Richard J. Correnti for making it my profession.

I am deeply grateful and appreciative of all the students I have counseled throughout the years. You have no idea how much you taught, challenged and inspired me. Without you, this book would not have been possible or necessary.

To my editors, Christine Belleris and Joseph Zolner, thank you for agreeing to bring your expertise to these pages.

And finally, I am eternally grateful to all my helpers, visible and invisible, who work behind the scenes on my behalf.

Preface

I was sixteen when I graduated from high school on a Friday night. On Saturday morning I was off to college. I have vivid memories of Daddy driving me to the train station on Seventh Avenue. He didn't say much. After buying my ticket and checking my luggage we said our goodbyes. As I watched him get in the car, he turned around and said to me "Remember, you're on a mission." And then he drove off.

As I waited for the train I became puzzled. I had always done what Mother and Daddy told me to do (well, maybe not *always*), so when they *told* me I was going to college I knew I had no choice. After all, that's where my sisters went when they finished high school. But as hard as I tried to 'remember,' no one ever said anything to me about a "mission"—and it was too late to ask. I was left to figure it out myself, and I didn't have a clue.

It took me ten years to get my bachelor's degree. And more than three decades later, I find that high school students are still going to college just like me—clueless. They have no idea how hard college is, and what it takes to graduate.

Years ago, only low income, first-generation-in-college students were labeled "at risk" for flunking out or dropping out. Today, entire classes of first-year college students are labeled "at risk." Students who are undecided about a major are "at risk." Transfer students, commuter students, gifted and talented students, student-athletes and others are all "at risk"!

My hope is that this book will help you avoid being labeled "at risk." And as you walk across the stage to receive your degree, perhaps you will say to your parents what I said to mine as I recalled that sunny day at the train station: "Mission accomplished."

Introduction

Anyone who wants to attend college has access to some type of higher education, and each year more and more high school students express an interest in attending. While institutional access and student desire to attend college have increased, retention and graduation rates have declined. More students are getting into college, but fewer students are getting out.

To address this problem, numerous programs, services and courses designed to better prepare students for college have been implemented in high schools, colleges and communities across the country. These initiatives include publicly and privately funded in-school, after school, weekend, summer, for-credit, and non-credit programs and courses. The programs target all ages, races, ethnicities, cultures, genders and socio-economic levels. They have been implemented by professionals, paraprofessionals, volunteers, parents, relatives and peers. They provide counseling, supplemental instruction, test preparation, field trips, and some even feed, clothe and house program participants. Yet as valuable, necessary and effective as these programs may be, they don't reach everyone.

This book is the product of more than two decades of counseling and teaching high school and college students how to succeed in college. I wrote it because today's youth need help developing a realistic picture of what to expect, and what is expected of them when they attend college. And my experience as the instructor for the College Life Skills Course® has taught me that students don't want to be told what to do. Instead, they want to discover it for themselves. I cannot think of a better way to empower this generation than to provide the questions to be asked and let them take control.

The *College FAQ Book* is a non-threatening introduction to college. It provides detailed lists of thought-provoking questions to ask high school counselors, college officials and others *prior* to making decisions about college participation. It sheds light on how colleges work, for which students and with what resources. It helps you understand the choices, challenges, bridges and barriers that college students encounter. And it clarifies differences between what students *think* college is all about and what it is in *reality.*

There are no answers in this book. No two colleges are alike and no two students are alike. Make it your responsibility to become actively involved in seeking answers based on the characteristics of the institutions you choose and your individual preferences.

The book is organized into three parts: Questions in Part I focus on how to get into college. Questions in Part II deal with what happens when students are on campus. Questions in Part III address getting out of college and entering the workplace.

This book was written for high school students who want to go to college; those who are being forced to go to college; and those who would like to go to college but think they can't. Undergraduate and graduate students will also find it a useful reference as they progress through the college experience.

To gain the most from this book read everything first. Get the big picture. As you read, circle or highlight the questions that interest, intrigue, puzzle, surprise or astonish you. Some questions stand alone. Others must be asked in sequence and in context. Make your own list of follow-up questions. Then go on a treasure hunt, searching and re-searching for answers everywhere. Ask college officials, current students, alumni, parents, relatives, teachers, counselors, clergy and mentors. Read catalogs, books, pamphlets, brochures and flyers. Go to college fairs. Visit campuses on-line and on-site. Start a discussion group.

The beauty of this book is that it puts you in control. You can take your time, you can take it with you, and you can refer to it again and again. Have fun!

PART I

FAQ's About Getting Into College

"The important thing
is never to stop questioning."

Albert Einstein

Think of the college experience as an interlocking jigsaw puzzle. When buying a puzzle it is important to know the size you want to attempt, what picture or image appeals to you, and how much it costs. To prepare the puzzle for assembly, you must separate the edges from the interior pieces, and sort them into piles based on their similarities and differences. To put the puzzle together, you must connect one piece at a time.

Each topic in this book represents a separate pile of puzzle pieces. As a high school student, think of yourself as an 'edge' piece. You are on the outskirts of college looking in. Your grades and test scores may make you a "border line" student. You may be nervous, tense or edgy about your prospects for admission. But you need not be worried because having the answers to the following questions will give you a competitive edge.

High School Preparation

Self Profile

1. What do I want to do after I graduate from high school?
2. How am I going to support myself?
3. How will I support a family?
4. Why do I want to go to college?
5. What job would I like to have?
6. Does the job I want require an education beyond high school?
7. How will I benefit from attending college?
8. Will I earn more money with a college degree?
9. How will I know I am ready for college?
10. What academic and life skills will I need for college?
11. Do I enjoy learning?

12. Am I willing to work hard in school?
13. Do I want a college degree?
14. Do I have an idea of what I want to study in college?

Career Exploration

15. What do I need to know about different careers?
16. How are careers classified?
17. How are occupational groups classified?
18. Are my favorite subjects related to specific career fields?
19. Are my hobbies related to specific career fields?
20. Are my skills and talents related to specific career fields?
21. Which high school electives are related to my career interests?
22. Do I want to pursue a career that enables me to interact with people?

23. Do I want to pursue a career that enables me to work with information or data?

24. Do I want to pursue a career that enables me to work with objects, machines, or outdoors?

25. Do I want to pursue a career that enables me to help improve others' lives?

26. Do I want to pursue a career that involves working in an office, keeping records and doing computations?

27. Do I want to pursue a career that involves works of art, literature, music, dance or theatre?

28. How will I know which academic major to pursue in college?

29. Which academic majors are related to my career interests?

30. Do I have the academic background required for my intended major?

31. Does my intended major require many science courses?

32. Does my intended major require many advanced math courses?
33. Does my intended major require many reading, writing and speaking courses?
34. Does my intended major require many English, history, psychology, economics or political science courses?
35. Does my intended major require many music, art, dance or drama courses?
36. What are the day-to-day working conditions for people in my intended major?
37. What do employees like or dislike about working in my intended major?
38. How many hours per week do employees work? At what times of the day?
39. Do employees work in shifts?
40. Do employees work during certain seasons?
41. Are employees required to travel as part of their work?

42. Do employees work outdoors? Indoors?

43. How can I visit places where people in my intended major work?

44. Which specific jobs are related to my intended major?

45. Where can I find descriptions of jobs related to my intended major?

46. What are the future job prospects for people in my intended major?

47. Are jobs in my intended major expected to grow or decline? How quickly or slowly?

48. How much do people working in my intended major earn annually?

49. What opportunities for advancement are available in my intended major?

50. Which extracurricular activities relate to my intended major?

51. Which high school clubs and activities are related to my intended major?

52. Which volunteer opportunities are related to my intended major?

53. Which academic contests or talent recognition competitions are related to my intended major?

54. What should I do in the summer to prepare for college?

55. How can I find a summer or part-time job that is related to my intended major?

56. What career resources are available to me in high school?

57. Who can I ask about career exploration?

58. Does my high school have a career counselor?

59. Do I need to make an appointment for career counseling?

60. Are career days scheduled at my high school?

61. Are job fairs scheduled in my community?

62. What can I read about career exploration?

63. What else should I know about exploring careers?

School Profile

64. What do colleges want to know about my high school?

65. Is my high school accredited? By which accrediting body?

66. Is my high school public?

67. Is my high school private?

68. Is my high school religious or parochial?

69. Is my high school a magnet school?

70. Is my high school a charter school?

71. Is my high school a home school?

72. Does my high school use a block schedule?

73. What library resources are available at my high school?

74. What computer resources are available at my high school?

75. What is my high school's minimum passing grade? 60? 65? 70? Other?

76. Does my high school use a ranking system?

77. How many teachers are certified in the subjects they teach?

78. How many of my teachers are teaching in their fields of expertise?

79. How many of my teachers are beginning teachers?

80. How many of my teachers have master's degrees?

81. How many of my teachers have specialist degrees?

82. How many of my teachers have doctoral degrees?

83. What is the racial, ethnic and second language makeup of my high school's teaching staff?

84. What is the racial, ethnic and second language makeup of my high school's student body?

85. How many students in my high school receive free or reduced lunches?

86. How many students speak English as a second language?

87. How do my high school's standardized test scores compare to the national average?

88. How many students from my high school go directly to vocational or technical schools?

89. How many students from my high school go directly to college after graduation?

90. How many students from my high school go directly to the workplace?

91. How many students from my high school go directly to the military?

92. How many students drop out of my high school?

93. How many students earn a standard diploma?

94. How many students earn an alternative diploma?

95. How many students earn a certificate of completion?

96. Does my high school require community service for graduation?

97. Does my high school require me to pass a statewide competency test?

98. Who can I ask about the courses needed to get into college?

99. Does my high school have guidance counselors?

100. What is the guidance counselor caseload?

101. Does my high school have a counselor specifically designed to help me apply to college?

102. What is my high school code for standardized tests?

103. Who can I talk to about my high school's characteristics?

104. What can I read about my high school's characteristics?

105. What else do colleges want to know about my high school?

Courses

106. Which high school courses do I need to get into this college?

107. Does my high school offer the courses I need to enter college?

108. Does my high school offer the courses I need to pursue my intended major?

109. How many required credits do I need to get into this college?

110. How many elective credits do I need to get into this college?

111. Which high school electives should I take?

112. Are the college requirements the same if I am home-schooled?

113. Which English courses do I need?
114. Which mathematics courses do I need?
115. Which science courses do I need?
116. Which social studies courses do I need?
117. Which foreign language courses do I need?
118. Am I exempt from a language requirement in college if my native language is not English?
119. Which visual and performing arts courses do I need?
120. Which health or fitness courses do I need?
121. Which computer courses do I need?
122. Do I need to take honors classes to get into this college?
123. Can I earn college credit by taking examinations?
124. If I earn credit by taking exams will I be able to graduate from college more quickly?

125. Will advanced placement classes in high school provide an opportunity to earn credit by examination?

126. What is the name of the exam(s) I can take?

127. How many exams must I pass to be eligible for advanced standing?

128. Does this college administer its own advanced placement exams?

129. Will enrollment in an international honors program give me advanced standing?

130. What is the maximum number of college credits I can earn by taking exams?

131. What can I do if these courses or programs are not offered at my high school?

132. When does this college begin to calculate my high school grade point average?

133. How can I make sure the credits I earned are recorded on my high school transcript?

134. What else can I do in high school to better prepare for this college?

135. Who can I ask to help me select courses that will meet college entrance requirements?

136. What can I read about how to select my high school courses?

137. What else should I know about high school courses that are required by this college?

Academic Skills

138. Which academic skills do I need to be successful in college?

139. How can I learn to read and comprehend written work at the college level?

140. How can I learn to write in English at the college level?

141. How can I learn to listen at the college level?

142. How can I learn to observe at the college level?

143. How can I learn to speak, or have a conversation about my course subject matter at the college level?

144. How can I learn to solve mathematical problems at the college level?

145. How can I learn to draw conclusions from written, spoken or graphic information at the college level?

146. How can I learn to distinguish between fact and opinion at the college level?

147. How can I learn to use a computer to enter, collect and retrieve information?

148. Who can I ask about learning college level academic skills?

149. What should I read to better understand the academic skills I will need in college?

150. What else should I know about academic skills for college?

Study Habits

151. What study habits must I develop in high school?

152. Should I make going to class a regular habit?

153. Where is the best place to sit in class?

154. Should I form the habit of taking notes in class?

155. What is the best way to take notes in class?

156. Do I need a folder or notebook for each class?

157. How should my folder or notebook be organized?

158. Should I form the habit of paying attention in class?

159. Should I form the habit of keeping up with my assignments?

160. What is the best way to keep up with my assignments?

161. Should I form the habit of asking questions in class?

162. Should I form the habit of following a routine study schedule?

163. How do I develop a study schedule?

164. When is the best time for me to study?

165. Should I form the habit of setting specific grade goals at the beginning of each grading period?

166. Should I form the habit of prioritizing what I need to study?

167. How do I prioritize what I need to study?

168. Should I form the habit of studying in a quiet place?

169. Where is the best place for me to study?

170. How can I avoid being distracted when I study?

171. Should I form the habit of studying in a well-lighted area?

172. What kind of lighting should I have in my study area?

173. Should I form the habit of studying in a well-ventilated area?

174. Which educational materials and supplies should I have in my study area?

175. Should I form the habit of doing my homework and other assignments daily?

176. What should I do when I sit down to study?

177. Should I form the habit of previewing or looking at an entire assignment first?

178. Should I form the habit of writing down any questions I have about an assignment?

179. Should I form the habit of reading an assignment word for word? How many times?

180. How can I remember what I study?

181. Should I form the habit of periodically reviewing my assignments to remember them?

182. Should I form the habit of making flash cards or summary sheets to better remember assignments?

183. Should I form the habit of asking for help with my assignments?

184. Is there a homework club in my high school?

185. Can I get help with homework online? Is it free?

186. Should I form the habit of turning my assignments in on time?

187. How can I prepare for tests, quizzes and exams?

188. Who can I ask about improving my study habits?

189. What can I read about improving my study habits?

190. What else should I know about developing good study habits?

Parent Profile

191. How can my parents help me prepare for college?

192. When will my parents talk to me about what I want to do in the future?

193. When will my parents talk to me about going to college?

194. Where can my parents get information about my options after high school?

195. Where can my parents get information about the different types of academic programs offered in my high school?

196. How will my parents know if my academic program in high school meets college admission requirements?

197. Where can my parents get information that will help me develop an academic plan?

198. How can my parents get involved in helping select my courses?

199. Will my parents help me select my ninth grade courses when I am in eighth grade?

200. Will my parents know when grade reports are issued?

201. Will my parents know how to calculate my grade point average?

202. Will my parents know the names of my teachers?

203. Will my parents know the name of my counselor?

204. Will my parents know the names of my school administrators?

205. How frequently will my parents visit my high school?

206. Will my parents schedule meetings with my teachers, counselors and administrators?

207. Will my parents get involved in high school programs and activities?

208. Will my parents attend parent association meetings?

209. Will my parents serve on high school advisory committees?

210. Will my parents attend open houses?

211. Will my parents ask me what I am learning in school?

212. Will my parents ask me how I feel about what I am learning in school?

213. Will my parents ask me if I enjoy what I am learning?

214. Will my parents ask me about the significance of what I am learning?

215. Will my parents ask me what skills I am developing?

216. Will my parents talk with me about their own educational experiences?

217. Will my parents talk with me about their own careers?

218. Will my parents make sure I have the equipment and supplies I need?

219. Will my parents make sure I have access to a computer?

220. Will my parents know how many hours of homework are assigned daily? Weekly?

221. Will my parents monitor how much time I spend socializing?

222. Will my parents make sure I study at a certain time each day?

223. Will my parents encourage me to use an academic planner to get organized?

224. Will my parents help me remember commitments and deadlines?

225. Will my parents help me with my homework?

226. Will my parents help me find tutoring or outside help if I need it?

227. Will my parents review my homework?

228. Will my parents encourage me to get involved in extracurricular activities?

229. Will my parents rely solely on high school personnel to get me into college?

230. Where can my parents obtain information on the procedures and deadlines for applying to college?

231. Where can my parents obtain information on the procedures and deadlines for applying for financial aid?

232. Where can my parents get information on what college scholarships students from my high school received in the past?

233. How will my parents know what information and documents they must provide on an admissions or financial aid application?

234. What influence will my parents have on where I go to college?

235. How early will my parents and I begin to save money for college?

236. Will I be able to go to college if my parents have never attended college?

237. Will I be able to go to college if my parents cannot afford to pay for college?

238. Who can my parents ask about preparing me for college?

239. What can my parents read about preparing me for college?

240. What else do my parents need to know about preparing me for college?

Early Access Programs

241. Are there dual- or joint-enrollment programs for high school students at this college?

242. Are there after-school enrichment programs at this college?

243. Are there summer enrichment programs at this college?

244. How are these programs funded?

245. How can I find out if I am eligible for these programs?

246. What grade do I have to be in to participate?
247. What family income requirements must I meet?
248. Are there citizenship requirements I must meet?
249. Do I have to provide proof of immunization?
250. Will I get paid during the program?
251. Can I participate if I have been home-schooled?
252. How do I obtain an application?
253. Is there an application fee?
254. When is the application deadline?
255. Do I have to take a test to qualify?
256. Do I have to write an essay?
257. Do I need a recommendation from my high school or teacher to participate?
258. Is parental permission required?

259. How will I be notified if I am accepted?
260. What high school activities will I be able to participate in?
261. What college activities will I be able to participate in?
262. Will I be able to enroll in college courses?
263. Which college courses can I take?
264. How many college courses can I take?
265. Do I have to register for the college courses in person?
266. Can I register for the college courses online?
267. Do I have to buy my own textbooks for the college courses?
268. Will the college courses duplicate my high school classes?
269. Will my college tuition and fees be waived?
270. Will my college credits count toward high school graduation?

271. Do I have to take these courses for a grade?

272. Can I take these courses on a pass/fail basis?

273. If I fail a course will I have a low grade point average before I am even admitted?

274. What are the requirements to remain in the program?

275. How many absences are permitted?

276. Must I maintain a specific grade point average to remain in the program?

277. Does program participation guarantee I will be admitted to this college?

278. Does program participation make me eligible for any scholarships?

279. Will I follow the academic calendar of my high school or this college?

280. Will I follow the code of conduct of my high school or this college?

281. When is the program offered? Evenings? Weekends? Summers?

282. What does a typical program schedule look like?

283. Is the program offered on campus?

284. Am I required to live on campus?

285. If I must live on campus, how often does the program schedule permit me to go home?

286. Do I have to purchase my meals?

287. Are meals provided if I qualify for free or reduced lunches?

288. Is transportation to and from the program provided?

289. Will I be able to use my high school bus pass?

290. Will I be able to use my local bus pass?

291. Will I be able to drive to campus?

292. Will I need a parking decal?

293. Will I have to pay for a parking decal?

294. Will I have to park in a specific area?

295. Who can I ask about early access programs?

296. What can I read about early access programs?

297. Who is in charge of early access programs?

298. What else should I know about early access programs at this college?

Entrance Exams

299. Must I take a standardized test to be admitted to this college?

300. What is the name of the required test(s)?

301. Should I take the test in a certain grade?

302. What subject matter does the test cover?

303. Have there been any recent changes in the material covered on test?

304. How much time do I have to finish entire test?

305. Is the test administered in one day?

306. Is the test administered over several days?

307. Is the test divided into sections? How many?

308. How much time do I have for each section?

309. Is there a break between sections? When? How long?

310. How many questions are on the test?

311. How are the questions formatted? Multiple choice? Essay? Both?

312. How many reading comprehension questions are on the test?

313. Is there a word limit on the essay portion of the test?

314. How many math questions are on the test?

315. Are math formulas provided?

316. Can I use a calculator?

317. Which high school courses are needed to score well on the test?

318. Can the test be taken in my native language?

319. Can the test be taken on the computer?

320. Are the conditions for taking the test on the computer the same as on paper?

321. Are special testing accommodations provided to certain students? Which students? Under what conditions?

322. What special accommodations and equipment are provided?

323. Do special accommodations include additional time to complete the test? How much additional time?

324. Will scores earned with additional test time be reported individually or averaged with standard time scores?

325. Are practice tests available?

326. Should I take a test-prep course?

327. Where are test-prep courses offered?

328. What should I know about the background and experience of the provider of the test prep course?

329. How much do test-prep courses cost?

330. Should I ask the test prep course provider for references?

331. When are the test dates?

332. Are some dates more popular or crowded than others?

333. What if my religious beliefs prohibit Saturday or Sunday testing?

334. How do I obtain a test registration form?

335. Will I need my high school or college code to complete the form?

336. Are there multiple registration deadlines?

337. When is the early registration deadline?

338. When is the regular registration deadline?

339. When is the late registration deadline?

340. Can I change my test date after registering?

341. Is walk-in or stand-by registration permitted?

342. How much does it cost to take the test?

343. What form of payment is accepted? Money order? Check? Credit card?

344. Can I register and pay online? Does it cost more to pay online?

345. Will I have to pay any additional fees?

346. Will I have to pay a late fee?

347. Will I have to pay a special location fee?

348. Will I have to pay an extra fee to have my test hand-scored?

349. Will I have to pay an extra fee for standby registration?

350. Will I have to pay extra to have an additional report prepared?

351. Will I have to pay extra to have replacement scores prepared?

352. Will I have to pay extra for a non-Saturday test date?

353. Can I request a fee waiver? From whom? How?

354. Will I receive the fee waiver prior to the next test administration date?

355. When do I have to notify you if I am unable to take the test?

356. What is the test's refund policy?

357. Are fees received after the registration deadline refundable?

358. How long does it take to process a refund?

359. Where do I go to take the test?

360. How are test sites assigned?

361. What if I cannot find a local testing site?

362. Can I request a special testing location?

363. Are testing locations available in foreign countries?

364. If I register early, will I be assigned to my preferred testing site?

365. What are the directions to the test center?

366. What if I go to the wrong test center?

367. Can I make up a missed test?

368. Can I call the test center on my test date?

369. What is the phone number of my test center?

370. What time will phone coverage be provided?

371. How early should I arrive at the test center?

372. Will I be admitted if I arrive late?

373. What should I bring with me to the test?

374. What forms of identification are required to enter the test site?

375. How many forms of identification are needed?

376. Will I be photographed, fingerprinted or videotaped at the test site?

377. Do I need an admission ticket?

378. How many days before the test will I receive the admission ticket?

379. How will I receive the admission ticket? E-mail? Snail mail?

380. What if the information on my ticket is incorrect?

381. What should I do if I lose my ticket?

382. Is seating assigned at the test site or can I choose my own seat?

383. Can I bring food or drink into the test room?

384. If I have to leave the test room, will I be permitted to make up the missed time?

385. What should I do if I find an error or ambiguity in a test question?

386. What should I do if I have a complaint about the test center?

387. Can an administration of the test be cancelled or delayed? Under what circumstances?

388. How is this test scored? Manually? Electronically?

389. Are all of the test sections scored?

390. Is there a penalty for guessing if I don't know an answer?

391. How are test scores reported?

392. How do I interpret my scores?

393. How soon after the test date will I receive my scores?

394. Will I receive my scores in the mail? On the Internet? By telephone? Fax?

395. What if my scores don't arrive in the time frame specified?

396. How well do standardized test scores predict academic performance in college?

397. How well do different racial, ethnic, second language and gender groups perform on this test?

398. Can I take the test a second time?

399. How soon can I take the test again?

400. How many times can I repeat the test?

401. How does this college view taking the test multiple times?

402. Do students who take the test more than once usually increase their scores?

403. Will I be penalized by this college for submitting more than one test score?

404. Will my scores arrive in time for me to apply for early decision admissions?

405. Can the processing of my scores be rushed?

406. How do my scores compare with other students admitted to this college?

407. Do the test results tell me the areas I need to improve?

408. Will my scores be sent directly to the colleges I am interested in?

409. How many colleges can I chose to receive my scores?

410. What if I don't know where I want my scores to be sent?

411. Will I be able to change my score recipients after I register to take the test?

412. If I don't think I performed well, can my scores be cancelled? When? How?

413. Will my score recipients be notified that my scores were cancelled?

414. Will my scores automatically be sent anywhere else? Where? Why?

415. For what period of time are my scores valid?

416. Will this college accept a photocopy of my test score?

417. Will scoring well on this test put me on this college's mailing list?

418. Who can I ask about taking entrance exams?

419. What can I read about taking entrance exams?

420. What else should I know about entrance exams at this college?

Choosing a College

Types of Colleges

421. Is this a vocational, technical or trade school?

422. Is this a community or junior college?

423. Is this a liberal arts college?

424. Is this an historically black college?

425. Is this an Hispanic-serving college?

426. Is this a tribal college?

427. Is this a predominately-white college?

428. Is this a college of art, music, design or architecture?

429. Is this a college of business and management?

430. Is this a college of engineering and technology?

431. Is this a college of chiropractic, nursing, pharmacy or podiatry?

432. Is this a college of medicine?

433. Is this a theological seminary?

434. Is this a religious or faith-related college?

435. Is this a land-grant institution?

436. Is this a coed college?

437. Is this a women-only college?

438. Is this a men-only college?

439. Is this a maritime academy?

440. Is this a military institute?

441. Is this a culinary institute?

442. Is this a teacher's college?

443. Is this a law school?

444. What is this college's Carnegie classification?

445. Who can I ask about different types of colleges?

446. What can I read about different types of colleges?

447. What else should I know about this type of college?

Location and Surroundings

448. Where is this college located?

449. Is this location considered an urban, suburban or rural area?

450. Is this college located in a regional city? Small town?

451. What is the closest major city?

452. What is the population of the city?

453. How many miles away from my home is this college?

454. What is the time zone at this college?

455. What are the estimated travel costs from my home to this location?

456. What is the estimated travel time from my home to this location?

457. How often will I be able to go home if I attend this college?

458. Is a student discount available on commercial airlines, trains or buses?

459. How far away from this college is the airport, train or bus station?

460. Does this college pick students up from the airport, bus or train station?

461. How often will I be required to leave campus? Weekends? Breaks? Holidays?

462. What is the weather like at this college most of the year?

463. Does the campus ever close because of bad weather?

464. How will I be notified of a campus closure?

465. Will I need to wear any special clothing to live in this area?

466. What local health and safety considerations should I be aware of in this area?

467. What are the current levels of air pollution?

468. What are the current levels of noise pollution?

469. What is the water quality rating?

470. What neighborhoods surround the campus?

471. What is the crime rate in the surrounding neighborhoods?

472. Are college students welcome in the community?

473. What is there to do in the community?

474. Are there any tourist attractions in the community?

475. Are there any professional sports teams in the community?

476. Are grocery stores, shopping malls or entertainment centers within walking distance of the campus?

477. Are barber shops or hair salons within walking distance?

478. Are places of worship within walking distance?

479. Are local restaurants within walking distance?

480. What partnerships does this college have with the local community?

481. Do local businesses provide discounts to students?

482. Does this college have more than one campus? How many? How far away are they from each other?

483. What are the differences between the campuses?

484. Is the academic program I am interested in located on a branch campus?

485. Is it possible to complete my entire degree at a branch campus?

486. Who can I ask about this college's location and surroundings?

487. What can I read about this college's location and surroundings?

488. What else should I know about the location of this college?

Transportation

489. How do people get around in the community?

490. Where can I get a local map?

491. Is the community served by public transportation?

492. Which local bus, subway or train routes come on or near campus?

493. Are college students eligible for free or reduced fares on transportation?

494. Do taxicabs come on campus?

495. Are there carpool programs in the community?

496. Am I allowed to have a car on campus?

497. Must I register my car with campus police?

498. What are the pros and cons of having a car on campus?

499. How will I keep up with car maintenance?

500. Will I have to change my driver's license?

501. Will I have to change my license plates?

502. Will my car insurance policy have to change?

503. What should I do if I am in a car accident?

504. Is parking available on campus?

505. Is parking covered? Uncovered?

506. Do I need a parking decal?

507. Can a parking decal be used for more than one car?

508. Are there parking meters on campus?

509. Which coins do parking meters accept?

510. Is my parking permit valid in the surrounding neighborhood?

511. What are the rules for parking on campus?

512. Are parking tickets issued by campus police?

513. How much are the fines for parking or moving violations?

514. Can I appeal a parking ticket?

515. Can I use faculty/staff parking spaces during evening hours?

516. Is emergency mechanical assistance available on campus?

517. Can I leave my car on campus overnight?

518. How do students get around on campus?

519. How much time will I have between classes?

520. How far will I have to walk to get to class?

521. What is the average distance between buildings?

522. Where can I get a campus map?

523. Is there a free college shuttle service?

524. Is the shuttle service accessible to disabled students?

525. Does the shuttle service go to branch campuses?

526. Does the shuttle service go into town?

527. Do I need a pass or identification card to ride on the shuttle?

528. Are bicycles permitted on campus?

529. Are there bike paths on campus?

530. Is bicycle parking available?

531. Are skateboards, in-line skates, and scooters permitted on campus?

532. Who can I ask about transportation at this college?

533. What can I read about transportation at this college?

534. What else should I know about transportation at this college?

Academic Degree Programs

535. Why do students attend this college?

536. How is this college different from other colleges?

537. What is the academic reputation of this college?

538. Does this college specialize in a particular academic program?

539. How can I receive a catalog or bulletin?

540. Is the catalog available online?

541. Do I have to purchase the catalog?

542. What is the academic calendar at this college?

543. How many weeks are in an academic term?

544. How many terms are in an academic year?

545. Is this college on a quarter system?

546. Is this college on a semester system?

547. Is this college on a trimester system?

548. Is this college on a 4-1-4 system?

549. Does this college award vocational certificates?

550. Does this college award academic degrees?

551. Which undergraduate degrees are conferred by this college?

552. Are associate of arts degrees awarded?

553. Are associate of science degrees awarded?

554. Are bachelor's degrees awarded?

555. Which graduate degrees are conferred by this college?

556. Are master's degrees awarded?

557. Are specialist degrees awarded?

558. Are doctoral degrees awarded?

559. Are professional degrees awarded?

560. Can I conduct postdoctoral research at this college?

561. Can I earn a certificate or get certified in specific academic areas?

562. Is this college ranked by any magazines or newspapers?

563. Is this college ranked by any other organizations?

564. Which academic programs have the largest enrollments?

565. Which academic majors are offered?

566. Are there any special study options available at this college?

567. Is a self-designed major available?

568. Is study-abroad available?

569. Is a domestic student-exchange program an option?

570. Are learning communities an option?

571. Do students in learning communities take their classes together?

572. Are weekend and evening programs available?

573. Are joint-degree programs with other institutions offered?

574. Can I earn bachelor's and master's degrees simultaneously?

575. Can I earn master's and doctoral degrees simultaneously?

576. Can I have a major in one department and a minor in the same or a different department?

577. Can I have two majors in the same or a different department?

578. Can I earn Bachelor of Arts and

Bachelor of Science degrees simultaneously?

579. How many students complete more than one major?

580. Is my intended major accredited by a national or professional organization? Which one(s)?

581. Will a degree from this college be accepted by employers in my field?

582. Who can I ask about academic programs at this college?

583. What can I read about academic programs at this college?

584. Who is in charge of the academic programs I am interested in?

585. What else should I know about the academic programs at this college?

Faculty Profile

586. Who teaches courses at this college?

587. What are the qualifications of faculty members?

588. Are faculty recruited from academia, industry or both?

589. Are faculty well known for their research?

590. Are faculty well known for their teaching?

591. Are faculty well known for being accessible to students?

592. What attracts faculty to work at this college?

593. What makes faculty want to stay at this college?

594. How many members of the faculty are professors?

595. How many are associate professors?

596. How many are assistant professors?

597. How many are visiting scholars?

598. How many are adjunct instructors?

599. How many are lecturers?

600. How many are teaching assistants?

601. How many are graduate assistants?

602. How many faculty in my intended major are full-time? Part-time?

603. How many faculty members in my intended major have doctoral degrees?

604. How many faculty members in my intended major have master's degrees?

605. How many faculty members in my intended major have tenure?

606. How many faculty members in my intended major are being reviewed for tenure?

607. How many faculty members in my intended major are at the rank of full professor?

608. What is the racial, ethnic, gender and second language make-up of faculty members in my intended major?

609. What is the average salary for part-time instructors?

610. What is the average salary for nine-month faculty in my intended major?

611. What is the average salary for twelve-month faculty in my intended major?

612. What is the student/faculty ratio in my intended major?

613. How many classes do faculty members in my intended major teach each term?

614. How many students do faculty members in my intended major advise each term?

615. What is the preferred teaching style at this college?

616. Do professors actively involve students in learning? How?

617. Do professors primarily lecture?

618. Do professors include group discussions in their teaching?

619. Do professors include role-plays in their teaching?

620. Do professors include case studies in their teaching?

621. Do professors schedule guest speakers in their classes?

622. Do professors use the Socratic method of instruction?

623. Do professors use visual aids? Handouts? Overheads? Videos? Music?

624. Who are the most popular professors in my intended major?

625. How much personal attention do students receive from faculty in my intended major?

626. How can I find publications authored by faculty in my intended major?

627. Are faculty members involved in professional associations?

628. Are faculty members involved with businesses and corporations?

629. How often do faculty members go on leaves of absence?

630. Who can I ask about the faculty at this college?

631. What can I read about the faculty at this college?

632. Who is in charge of the faculty at this college?

633. What else should I know about the faculty at this college?

Governance Structure

634. How does this institution receive its funds?

635. Is this a for-profit or a nonprofit college?

636. Is this a public or private college?

637. Is this college licensed or approved by the city or state in which it is located?

638. Is this college accredited by a regional accrediting agency?

639. Is this college accredited by a specialized accrediting body?

640. Is this college accredited by a national accrediting body?

641. Is the accrediting agency recognized by the federal government?

642. How old is this college?

643. How did this college get its name?

644. What is this college's history?

645. What is the meaning or significance of this college's logo, emblem or insignia?

646. Is this college affiliated with any other organization?

647. What is this college's mission statement or philosophy?

648. Who are the members of the college's board of trustees?

649. Are trustees appointed or elected?

650. Are there any other major governing boards or committees?

651. What is the market value of this college's endowment?

652. How does this college invest its money?

653. Is this college currently under sanction by any organization?

654. Has this college's accreditation been threatened?

655. Has this college considered closing recently?

656. Have there been any recent negative media reports about this college?

657. Have there been any recent budget cuts? Where? Why?

658. Have any programs of study been eliminated? Why?

659. Have any faculty positions been cut? Why?

660. How much funding does this college receive from private sources?

661. How much funding does this college receive from government sources?

662. How much funding does this college receive from contracts and grants?

663. How much college research is

commercially- or corporate-sponsored?

664. What influence, if any, do commercial sponsors have on research activities?

665. Where can I review the college's budget?

666. How much of the budget goes to the academic units?

667. How much of the budget goes to the academic department for my intended major?

668. How much is spent annually on student support services?

669. How much is spent annually on operations and maintenance?

670. How much is spent annually on scholarships and other student financial awards?

671. How much is spent annually on auxiliary enterprises?

672. How much is spent annually on public service?

673. Who is the president or chancellor of this college?

674. How long has the president been in office?

675. Does the president schedule office hours to meet with students?

676. How can I review this college's organizational chart?

677. Which administrators report directly to the president?

678. Who are the vice presidents or vice chancellors at this college?

679. Who is the dean of students?

680. Who is the provost of the faculty?

681. Is this institution a university?

682. Which academic programs are organized into colleges?

683. Which academic programs are organized into schools or departments?

684. Which academic programs are organized into centers or institutes?

685. Who is the dean of the college or school that offers my intended major?

686. Who is the chairperson of my academic department?

687. Who is the ombudsperson?

688. Who is the equal opportunity program administrator?

689. How many employees are permanent full-time?

690. How many employees are permanent part-time?

691. How many employees are male? Female?

692. What is the employee breakdown by race, second language and ethnicity?

693. How many employees have doctoral, master's or bachelor's degrees?

694. How many employees are clerical support staff?

695. How many employees are custodians and maintenance workers?

696. Are faculty members represented by a labor union?

697. Are any other employees represented by a labor union?

698. Who can I ask about the governance structure of this college?

699. What can I read about the governance structure of this college?

700. What else should I know about the governance structure at this college?

Student Profile

General

701. How many students attend this college?

702. How many are first year college students?

703. How many are transfer students?

704. How many are undergraduate students?

705. How many are graduate students?

706. How many students are unclassified?

707. How many students are non-degree-seeking?

708. How many students are full-time?

709. How many students are part-time?

710. What is the average high school grade point average for first year students?

711. How many students were valedictorians?

712. How many students were salutatorians?

713. How many students attended public high schools?

714. How many students attended private high schools?

715. How many graduated in the top 10 percent of their high school classes?

716. How many graduated in the top 25 percent of their high school classes?

717. How many graduated in the top 50 percent of their high school classes?

718. How many graduated in the lower half of their high school classes?

719. What is the average entrance exam score for first year students?

720. What is the average entrance exam score for graduate students?

721. What is the average age of students at this college?

722. How many students are twenty-five and older?

723. How many students work full time?

724. How many students have children?

725. How many students already have a bachelor's degree?

726. How many students are male?

727. How many students are female?

728. What are the racial, ethnic and second language makeups of the student body?

729. What is the religious makeup of the student body?

730. What is the average household income of the student body?

731. How many students are from in state?

732. How many students are from out of state?

733. How many students are from other countries?

734. How many students live on campus?

735. How many students commute to campus?

736. How many students leave this college after the first year? What are their reasons for leaving?

737. How many students leave voluntarily?

738. How many students leave involuntarily?

739. How long does it take undergraduate students to graduate?

740. How many students graduate in four years?

741. How many students graduate in six years?

742. Does this college conduct exit interviews?

743. Does this college administer satisfaction surveys?

744. Where can I find the results of exit interviews and satisfaction surveys?

745. Who can I ask about current students?

746. What can I read about current students?

747. Who is in charge of student development programs?

748. How can I contact current students?

749. Where are student development program offices located?

750. When are student development program offices open? Evenings? Weekends?

751. What else should I know about students who attend this college?

Athletes

752. How many students at this college are athletes?

753. Does this college belong to a national athletic association?

754. Are the eligibility requirements the same for all athletic associations?

755. How is this college's athletic program classified? Division I, II or III?

756. Are the academic requirements the same for all divisions?

757. Does this college belong to an athletic conference? Which one?

758. Has this college violated any athletic association rules or regulations?

759. Is this college currently under sanction by any athletic organizations?

760. Which intercollegiate sports are offered at this college?

761. How do I become eligible to play?

762. Is the college application process different for student athletes? How?

763. Do I have to complete any forms in addition to my college application?

764. Do I have to pay an eligibility processing fee?

765. Do I have to be recruited by a coach to play on a team?

766. When are coaches permitted to contact me?

767. Are boosters permitted to contact me?

768. Are the eligibility requirements the same for all sports?

769. Are eligibility requirements the same for all athletes?

770. Must I sign a letter of intent to play at this college?

771. How many seasons am I eligible to play?

772. What happens if I decide to take a term off?

773. Are athletic scholarships available?

774. Can all divisions offer scholarships?

775. How long are scholarships valid?

776. Are scholarships valid in the summer term?

777. What happens to my scholarship if I am injured?

778. What medical assistance is provided if I am injured?

779. Is there a maximum amount of financial aid that athletes may receive?

780. Under what circumstances can my scholarship be cancelled or reduced?

781. What are the requirements for satisfactory academic progress for athletes?

782. What is the minimum grade point average required for athletes to remain eligible to compete?

783. What is the minimum number of credit hours athletes must earn each term?

784. Are student athletes able to work on and off campus?

785. How quickly will I be able to practice or compete?

786. How often do student athletes practice?

787. Are practices limited to a certain number of hours per day or per week?

788. How often do student athletes travel?

789. What is the class attendance policy for athletes?

790. What property, facilities and equipment are available to student athletes?

791. How well maintained are the properties, facilities and equipment or athletes?

792. Which intramural sports are offered at this college?

793. Are intramural sports clinics, lessons or workshops offered?

794. What are the requirements for participating in intramural sports?

795. Does this college prepare a report on gender equity in athletics?

796. Does this college prepare a report on the graduation rates of athletes by race?

797. Where can I locate copies of the gender and graduation rate reports?

798. Are athletes required to live on campus?

799. Do student athletes live separately from other students on campus?

800. Are student athletes required to attend study hall, tutoring or counseling sessions?

801. Are student athletes subject to the same academic standards as other students?

802. Is there a separate code of conduct for student athletes?

803. Am I immediately ineligible to play if I violate the code of conduct?

804. Am I required to take drug tests?

805. Will I be randomly selected to take a drug test?

806. Will failing a drug test jeopardize my eligibility?

807. Is help available if I have a drug or banned substance addiction?

808. If I transfer to another school do I have to notify my new college I tested positive for a banned substance?

809. Do I have to provide authorization to the athletic department to disclose my educational records for publication?

810. Do I have to provide authorization for my name and photograph to appear in college publicity materials?

811. What are the advantages and disadvantages of being a student athlete?

812. What are the most common mistakes that student athletes make when applying to this college?

813. What services are provided to student athletes?

814. Who can I ask about student athletes?

815. What can I read about student athletes?

816. Who is in charge of the athletic program?

817. How can I contact current student athletes?

818. Where is the athletics program office located?

819. When is the athletics program office open? Evenings? Weekends?

820. What else should I know about student athletes at this college?

Disabled Students

821. How many learning disabled students attend this college?

822. How many physically disabled students attend this college?

823. What documentation is needed to verify a disability?

824. Who should prepare my disability documentation?

825. Will documenting my disability hurt my chances of gaining admission?

826. How often must I submit disability documentation?

827. Does this college have a disability compliance officer?

828. Will my professors be notified that I have a disability?

829. What accommodations are made for disabled students?

830. What specialized equipment is provided at this college?

831. Do disabled students receive priority when registering for classes?

832. What special accommodations are made for visually impaired students?

833. Are readers made available to visually impaired students?

834. Are note-takers made available?

835. Are oral interpreters provided?

836. Is a Braille version of course materials made available?

837. Is there a device available on campus for enlarging print?

838. Are variable-speed tape recorders provided?

839. Can my classes be tape-recorded?

840. Can my course materials be put on audiotape?

841. Can I have a guide dog on campus?

842. Can my guide dog live with me on campus?

843. What special accommodations are made for hearing-impaired students?

844. Does this college provide sign-language interpretation?

845. Is there a telephone communication device (TDDY) available for the deaf?

846. Is a voice synthesizer provided?

847. Are assistive-listening devices provided?

848. Do on-campus television stations provide closed captioning for the hearing impaired?

849. What special accommodations are made for students who are learning disabled?

850. Does this college have special sections of required courses for students with learning disabilities?

851. Are library aides provided?

852. Are alternative testing arrangements made for disabled students?

853. Can class tests be taken orally?

854. Can the test be read to disabled students?

855. Can someone write test answers for disabled students?

856. Can exams be tape-recorded?

857. Can exams be given in Braille?

858. Can exams be given in enlarged print?

859. Can answer sheets be provided in enlarged print?

860. Are additional testing and study breaks permitted?

861. Is additional testing time permitted?

862. How much additional time is provided? Time and a half? Double time?

863. Is a separate testing room provided?

864. Is special lighting provided?

865. Is an adjustable table/chair provided?

866. Is a printed copy of spoken test directions provided?

867. For computer-based tests, am I able to select the background and foreground colors?

868. Is a special mouse or special keyboard provided?

869. Are all facilities, buildings, offices and classrooms wheelchair accessible?

870. Are all doors equipped with automatic-opening devices?

871. Are restrooms, water fountains, elevators and corridors accessible to wheelchairs?

872. Are wheelchair-bound students able to move around campus unaided?

873. Is mobility training provided? When?

874. Does this college's evacuation policy accommodate and address persons in wheelchairs?

875. What is the emergency exit procedure for blind students?

876. Are strobe or buzzer fire alarms used in emergencies to alert the hearing impaired?

877. Can a personal assistant attend classes with a disabled student?

878. What if an interpreter, note-taker, reader or library aide does not show up?

879. Is disabled parking available on campus?

880. Do I need a special parking permit from this college in addition to my state-issued tag?

881. Can I discontinue my relationship with disability services at any time?

882. Can I volunteer to help disabled students on campus?

883. What are the most common mistakes made by disabled applicants?

884. Who can I ask about disabled students at this college?

885. What can I read about disabled students?

886. Who is in charge of disabled student services?

887. How can I contact current disabled students?

888. How can I contact the disabled student office?

889. Where is the disabled student office located?

890. When is the disabled student office open? Evenings? Weekends?

891. What else should I know about students with disabilities at this college?

Honor Students

892. How many honor students are there at this college?

893. Do I have to be invited to participate in the honors program?

894. Why should I participate in the honors program?

895. Do I have to complete a separate honors program application?

896. What are the entrance requirements?

897. What are the requirements to stay in the honors program?

898. Is a higher high school grade point average required to participate in the honors program?

899. Is a higher standardized test score required to participate in the honors program?

900. If I enrolled in the honors program will all my courses be honors courses?

901. What will I study in the honors program?

902. How many honors classes do I have to take?

903. Are honors courses more difficult than non-honors courses?

904. Am I required to write an honors thesis?

905. Is the honors program compatible with my intended major?

906. What minimum GPA do I have to maintain?

907. Will being in the honors program lower my GPA?

908. Is there a non-graded option for honors courses?

909. Am I required to live in specific housing for honor students?

910. Are there any special scholarships for honor students?

911. Does advanced placement credit apply toward honors course requirements?

912. Am I required to travel abroad if enrolled in the honors program?

913. When do I have to let this college know that I accept admission into the honors program?

914. Can I enter the honors program in my second year?

915. What should I do if no honors courses fit my schedule?

916. Can I take an honors independent study?

917. Is there a separate lounge or facility for honor students?

918. Can transfer students join the honors program?

919. Will my honors credits transfer to another institution?

920. Will the honors program help me get a better job after graduation?

921. What are the advantages and disadvantages of being an honors student?

922. What are the most common mistakes honors program applicants make?

923. What additional program services are provided to honors students?

924. Who can I ask about honors students?

925. What can I read about honors students?

926. Who is in charge of the honors program?

927. How can I contact current honor students?

928. Where is the honors program office located?

929. When is the honors program office open? Evenings? Weekends?

930. What else should I know about honors students at this college?

International Students

931. Which countries do most international students come from to attend this college?

932. What additional application information is required of international students?

933. Is the application deadline the same for international students? Earlier?

934. Am I required to take a language proficiency test?

935. Do the high school requirements I have completed in my country have to be the same as this college's high school requirements?

936. Must my high school transcript be evaluated?

937. Am I required to use a specific evaluation service? Which one?

938. How much does it cost for my transcript to be evaluated?

939. How long does it take for a transcript to be evaluated?

940. Must the evaluation service receive my documents in their original language?

941. Must the translation be certified?

942. Must I provide a course description of what was covered in each subject?

943. What happens if I disagree with the evaluation?

944. How much is tuition for international students?

945. Does this college offer scholarships for international students?

946. Does this college offer tuition waivers for international students?

947. Is nonfederal financial aid available to international students?

948. Do I have to certify that I have savings, scholarship, government or employer funds available to study in the United States?

949. What should I know about the foreign currency exchange?

950. Is there a language policy or language pledge at this college?

951. Can my family come to the United States with me?

952. Do I have to certify additional funds for my family?

953. Will my family be permitted to work while in the U.S.?

954. Will I be required to live on campus?

955. Can I live with a relative?

956. Must my relative be a permanent resident?

957. Does this college conduct a special orientation program for international students?

958. Does this college provide help to identify resources for my dietary, health care and language needs?

959. Is there an international student organization on campus?

960. Is there an international student health insurance requirement?

961. Can a health insurance policy from my country be used?

962. Am I required to carry repatriation coverage on my insurance policy?

963. Which documents from this college

will be needed to enter the United States to study?

964. Will a passport be needed?

965. Will a specific type of immigration card be needed?

966. Will a visa be needed?

967. What type of student visa will I receive?

968. What happens if I am denied a student visa?

969. What happens if my student visa expires?

970. Can I change my immigration status after I am in the United States?

971. After I enroll, what information about me will be reported to immigration?

972. Will I be required to notify the college of any address changes?

973. Will I be required to study full-time?

974. Will modifying my course load jeopardize my immigration status?

975. Can I take courses at another college in the United States?

976. Must I take the majority of my courses at this college?

977. Do I need approval to take classes at another college?

978. Will I be required to submit a transcript of classes taken at another college?

979. How much money should I bring to the United States? Cash? Traveler's checks? Credit cards?

980. Can I open a bank account in the United States and wire-transfer funds from my country?

981. Will I have to pay taxes in the United States?

982. Can I work on campus while I am in the United States?

983. Can I work off campus while I am in the United States?

984. Do I need a United States work permit to work on campus?

985. Will I receive help to comply with U.S. immigration laws?

986. Will I receive help re-entering or returning to my home country?

987. How often should I contact family and friends in my home country?

988. How long can I stay in the United States after I graduate?

989. Am I eligible for a practical training program?

990. When am I required to leave the U.S.?

991. What arrangements do I have to make if I want to travel to another country or return home?

992. Can this college make contact with an embassy on my behalf?

993. What are the advantages and disadvantages of being an international student?

994. What are the most common mistakes international student applicants make?

995. What services are provided to international students?

996. Who can I ask about international students?

997. What can I read about international students?

998. Who is in charge of international student services?

999. How can I contact current international students?

1000. Where is the international student office located?

1001. When is the international student office open? Evenings? Weekends?

1002. What else should I know about international students at this college?

Performing and Visual Artists

1003. How many students at this college are performing and visual artists?

1004. Is the application process different for performing and visual artists? How?

1005. How many students are studying art?

1006. How many students are studying music?

1007. How many students are studying theater?

1008. How many students are studying dance?

1009. Will I need to audition to be admitted to this college?

1010. Will I need to submit a portfolio of my work?

1011. Will I have to be interviewed?

1012. Will I need to have my own instrument?

1013. Will I have to pay for private lessons?

1014. Is studio space available on campus?

1015. Will I have to pay for extra for art supplies?

1016. Are there any requirements to continue in the program?

1017. What are the advantages and disadvantages of being a performing or visual arts student?

1018. What are the most common mistakes performing and visual artist applicants make?

1019. What services are provided to performing and visual artists?

1020. Who can I ask about performing and visual artist students?

1021. What can I read about performing and visual artist students?

1022. Who is in charge of the performing and visual artist programs?

1023. How can I contact current performing and visual artist students?

1024. Where is the performing and visual artist program office?

1025. When is the performing and visual artist program office open? Evenings? Weekends?

1026. What else should I know about performing and visual artist students at this college?

Returning Students

1027. Can I leave this college and return whenever I want?

1028. How will taking a term off affect my graduation schedule?

1029. What happens if I am not enrolled for a full academic year?

1030. Can I return if I am away for more than an academic year?

1031. Do I have to reapply if I have been out of this college for a few years?

1032. If I performed poorly in college years ago, can my past academic record be overlooked?

1033. Can I receive academic credit for my life experience?

1034. Can I create my own degree program based on my experience?

1035. How can I start taking classes again?

1036. Are credits earned in the military accepted?

1037. Can I take noncredit classes if I am seeking a degree? How many?

1038. Must I apply for admission if I only want to take noncredit courses?

1039. What are the advantages and disadvantages of being a returning student?

1040. For how long can academic credits be applied toward graduation requirements?

1041. What are the most common mistakes returning student applicants make?

1042. What services are provided to returning students?

1043. Who can I ask about returning students?

1044. What can I read about returning students?

1045. Who is in charge of returning student services?

1046. How can I contact currently enrolled returning students?

1047. How can I contact the returning student office?

1048. Where is the returning student office located?

1049. When is the returning student office open? Evenings? Weekends?

1050. What else should I know about returning students at this college?

Transfer Students

1051. How many students transfer to this college?

1052. How many students transfer out of this college?

1053. What is the procedure to transfer to this college?

1054. Will I be required to meet the admissions requirements for freshman or sophomores?

1055. Is the application deadline the same as for first-time applicants?

1056. Is there a transfer application fee?

1057. How many transfer credits can be accepted?

1058. Will vocational or technical college credits be accepted?

1059. If I have received an associate of arts degree, will I automatically enter this college as a junior?

1060. Can I complete less than sixty credits at this college and still be able to transfer?

1061. What is the lowest grade that can be transferred?

1062. How will I know which credits have been transferred?

1063. Are developmental course credits transferable?

1064. How are quarter hours converted to semester hours?

1065. Must transfer students retake entrance exams?

1066. Must transfer students retake placement tests?

1067. When is the best time to transfer to this college?

1068. What is the minimum number of credits I can complete to transfer to this college?

1069. Can I take courses at this college before being admitted as a transfer student?

1070. Can I take a few courses at another college before getting my degree from this college?

1071. Does this college have transfer or articulation agreements with other colleges? Which ones?

1072. Is a statement of good academic standing from my previous college required?

1073. Is a statement of good conduct from my previous college required?

1074. Will my prior financial aid awards automatically transfer to this college?

1075. What must be done to transfer my financial aid to this college?

1076. How different is this college from my previous college?

1077. Are the governance and administrative systems at both colleges the same?

1078. When do transfer students register for classes?

1079. Can transfer students live in on-campus housing?

1080. What are the advantages and disadvantages of being a transfer student?

1081. What are the most common mistakes transfer applicants make?

1082. What services are provided to transfer students?

1083. Who can I ask about transfer students?

1084. What can I read about transfer students?

1085. Who is in charge of transfer student services?

1086. How can I contact current transfer students?

1087. Where is the transfer student office located?

1088. When is the transfer student office open? Evenings? Weekends?

1089. What else should I know about transfer students at this college?

Veterans

1090. Does this college accept veterans education benefits?

1091. Does my intended major qualify for veterans benefits?

1092. What is the procedure for applying as a veteran?

1093. How long will it take to receive my veterans benefits?

1094. Are veterans education benefits taxable?

1095. What are the advantages and disadvantages of being a veteran student?

1096. What are the most common mistakes veteran applicants make?

1097. What services are provided to veteran students?

1098. Who can I ask about veteran students?

1099. What can I read about veteran students?

1100. Who is in charge of veteran services?

1101. How can I contact current veteran students?

1102. Where is the veteran students office located?

1103. When is the veteran students office open? Evenings? Weekends?

1104. What else should I know about veteran students at this college?

Student Life

1105. What do students at this college do when they are not studying?

1106. What do students at this college do for fun?

1107. Which clubs and organizations are available on campus?

1108. How many groups are volunteer service organizations?

1109. How many groups are political organizations?

1110. How many groups are cultural organizations?

1111. How many groups are religious organizations?

1112. How many groups are intramural or sports clubs?

1113. How many are honor societies?

1114. Which are the most popular organizations? Why?

1115. How many are fraternities and sororities?

1116. Is there a student government association?

1117. How do I get involved in student government?

1118. Which student government committees can I join?

1119. Is there a student activity committee or programming board?

1120. How can I organize an activity or event?

1121. How can I bring a speaker on campus?

1122. How can I work on a student publication?

1123. How can I obtain funding to start a club?

1124. Can clubs and organizations do their own fundraising?

1125. Do clubs and organizations have office space on campus?

1126. How can I find other students who may want to start a similar club?

1127. Must clubs have a faculty or staff advisor?

1128. What type of entertainment is provided on campus?

1129. What incentives exist for students to attend campus events? Free food? Give-aways?

1130. Must I pay to attend lectures, dances, concerts or other activities?

1131. What campus traditions exist at this college?

1132. Is a convocation ceremony held for new students?

1133. Is a homecoming celebration held?

1134. Is a welcome-back-to-campus celebration held?

1135. Is a Black History Month celebration held?

1136. Is a Cinco de Mayo celebration held?

1137. Is a Hispanic Heritage Month celebration held?

1138. Is a Jewish History Month celebration held?

1139. Is a Women's History Month celebration held?

1140. Do most students remain on campus on weekends?

1141. Where do students go on weekends?

1142. What do students do during spring break?

1143. Is there a student-run newspaper on campus?

1144. Is there a student-run radio or television station on campus?

1145. Is a yearbook published annually?

1146. Is there a film society?

1147. What is the political climate at this college?

1148. What is the athletic reputation of varsity teams at this college?

1149. What is the athletic reputation of intramural teams at this college?

1150. What is this college's nickname?

1151. What is the name of this college's mascot?

1152. What are this college's colors?

1153. Is there a marching band?

1154. Is there a symphony orchestra?

1155. Is there a cheerleading squad?

1156. Is there a dance group?

1157. Is there a flag-and-rifle corps?

1158. Is there a choral group on campus?

1159. Is there an inspirational or gospel choir on campus?

1160. Is there a drama or theater group?

1161. What are the words to the college alma mater?

1162. What are the words to the college fight song?

1163. What are the advantages and disadvantages of getting involved in student life?

1164. What assistance is available to students who plan events and activities?

1165. Who can I ask about student life?

1166. What can I read about student life?

1167. Who is in charge of student life programs?

1168. How can I contact students who are involved in student life programs?

1169. Where is the student life program office located?

1170. When is the student life program office open? Evenings? Weekends?

1171. What else should I know about student life at this college?

Student Support Services

1172. How does this college support students outside of the classroom?

1173. Is there a student development center on campus?

1174. Is there a campus ministry office?

1175. Is there a career services office?

1176. Is there a commuter student services office?

1177. Is there a counseling or mental health services office?

1178. Is there a disabled student services office?

1179. Is there a drug and alcohol addiction resource office?

1180. Is there a food service office?

1181. Is there a student employment office?

1182. Is there a gay, lesbian, bisexual or transgender office?

1183. Is there a fraternity and sorority office?

1184. Is there a health center, medical center or infirmary?

1185. Is there an internship or cooperative education office?

1186. Is there an international student office?

1187. Is there an ombudsperson office?

1188. Is there a judicial affairs office?

1189. Is there a legal services office?

1190. Is there a student mentoring program office?

1191. Is there a minority affairs office?

1192. Is there a multicultural affairs office?

1193. Is there an orientation program office?

1194. Is there a parking and traffic office?

1195. Is there a peer advisor or peer leader office?

1196. Is there a student activities office?

1197. Is there a student retention office?

1198. Is there a testing center?

1199. Is there a tutorial or learning resource center?

1200. Is there a veterans affairs office?

1201. Is there a victim advocacy office?

1202. Is there a volunteer or service learning center?

1203. Is there a women's resource office?

1204. What services does each office provide?

1205. Are student support services free to currently enrolled students?

1206. Who can I ask about student support services?

1207. What can I read about student support services?

1208. Who is in charge of student support services?

1209. How can I contact student support services offices?

1210. Where are student support services offices located?

1211. When are student support service offices open? Evenings? Weekends?

1212. What else should I know about student support services at this college?

Campus Facilities

1213. How many acres does the campus occupy?

1214. How many buildings are on campus?

1215. How are the buildings named, coded or organized?

1216. What are the buildings' nicknames?

1217. Who are the buildings named after?

1218. How much space is dedicated to classrooms?

1219. How much space is dedicated to teaching laboratories?

1220. Does my intended major require specialized labs or facilities?

1221. How much space is dedicated to study facilities?

1222. Is there a bookstore on campus?

1223. Is the bookstore college-owned or privately owned?

1224. Is there a math laboratory?

1225. Is there a reading laboratory?

1226. Is there a writing laboratory?

1227. Is there an instructional media center?

1228. Is there a multicultural center?

1229. Is there an art or ceramics studio?

1230. Are there any art museums or galleries on campus?

1231. Are residence halls located on campus? Off campus?

1232. Is there a childcare facility?

1233. Is there a conference center?

1234. Is there a teleconferencing center?

1235. Is there a grocery store or mini mart on campus?

1236. Is there a restaurant on campus?

1237. Is there a hotel on campus?

1238. Is there a theater or performing arts center on campus?

1239. Is there a student union or student center?

1240. Is there a bank on campus?

1241. Is there a barber shop or hair salon?

1242. Is there a bowling alley?

1243. Is there a barbecue pavilion?

1244. Is there a chapel, sanctuary, church, mosque or temple?

1245. Is there a copy center?

1246. Is there an instructional media center?

1247. Is there a dining hall?

1248. Is there a dry cleaner?

1249. Is there a music listening room?

1250. Is there a post office or mail center?

1251. Is there a ticket agency?

1252. Is there a travel agency?

1253. Is there a movie theater?

1254. Is there a wellness center?

1255. Is there a fitness, weight room or exercise center?

1256. Is there a game room?

1257. Is there a gymnasium on campus?

1258. Is there an athletic field house?

1259. Is there a baseball stadium?

1260. Is there a basketball court?

1261. Is there a track-and-field facility?

1262. Is there a dock on campus?

1263. Is there a football field?

1264. Is there a golf course?

1265. Is there a greenhouse?

1266. Is there a hockey center?

1267. Is there an obstacle or ropes course?

1268. Is there a soccer field?

1269. Is there a softball stadium?

1270. Is there a squash court?

1271. Is there a swimming pool?

1272. Is there a tennis court?

1273. Is there a volleyball court?

1274. Is there a preschool, elementary, middle or high school on campus?

1275. Is there a small business development center?

1276. Will I have access to all of these facilities on all campuses?

1277. Which facilities require me to pay an additional fee?

1278. If some of these facilities are not on campus, are they located nearby?

1279. Who can I ask about campus facilities?

1280. What can I read about campus facilities?

1281. Who is in charge of campus facilities?

1282. How can I contact the campus facilities office?

1283. Where is the campus facilities office located?

1284. When is the campus facilities office open? Evenings? Weekends?

1285. What else should I know about facilities at this college?

College Admission

College Fairs

1286. Do college recruiters ever visit my geographic area? When?

1287. Do recruiters at this college participate in college fairs?

1288. Which organizations sponsor college fairs?

1289. How do I find out when college fairs are being held in my area?

1290. Will my high school teacher or counselor notify me about upcoming fairs?

1291. Will I hear about college fairs on the high school announcements?

1292. Will I hear about fairs on the radio?

1293. Will I read about fairs in the newspaper?

1294. Will fair information appear on television?

1295. Will I receive an e-mail about a fair?

1296. When are college fairs typically scheduled? At what time?

1297. How many colleges typically participate in a college fair?

1298. Will the list of colleges attending the fair be available ahead of time?

1299. Will a fair map showing where college representatives are located be available?

1300. What happens at a college fair?

1301. What should I wear to a college fair?

1302. Will I be able to ask college representatives questions?

1303. How do I decide which college representatives to talk to?

1304. Which questions should I be prepared to answer?

1305. What should I bring to a college fair?

1306. Will workshops or information sessions be held at the fair? On which topics?

1307. Will college brochures or other materials and publications be available?

1308. Will financial aid representatives be available?

1309. Can I complete a college application at the fair?

1310. Will college representatives be able to tell me if I am admissible to their colleges?

1311. Will I be able to add my name to the college's mailing list?

1312. How will college representatives follow up with me after the fair?

1313. How soon will I receive any information I requested?

1314. How should I follow up with colleges I am interested in?

1315. What are the advantages and disadvantages of attending college fairs?

1316. Who can I ask about college fairs?

1317. What can I read about college fairs?

1318. How can I contact college fair organizers?

1319. What else should I know about college fairs?

Entrance Requirements

1320. What are the admissions requirements for degree-seeking students?

1321. Is a high school diploma required for admission?

1322. Is a general equivalency diploma (GED) accepted?

1323. Is a certificate of attendance diploma accepted?

1324. Is there a required college entrance examination score? What is the score?

1325. What is the high school grade point average requirement?

1326. Can entrance requirements be met through a combination of my grade point average and test scores?

1327. Is there a required class rank? What is the rank?

1328. Am I required to know what I want to major in before applying to this college?

1329. Do all academic programs at this college have the same admission requirements?

1330. If admitted to this college am I automatically admitted to my major?

1331. Does my intended major only accept a limited number of students?

1332. What are the requirements for academic majors in limited enrollment programs?

1333. Is a higher grade point average required for limited enrollment programs?

1334. Are higher test scores required for limited enrollment programs?

1335. Does this college require or prefer a special talent? Which one(s)?

1336. Is a resume, portfolio, audition tape or writing sample required for admission?

1337. Am I required to take a vision, hearing or speech-screening test?

1338. Am I required to take a physical exam?

1339. Will I have to take drug-screening tests?

1340. What are the citizenship and residency requirements for admission to this college?

1341. Are students who are married, pregnant or have dependents eligible for admission?

1342. Are any high school students who graduate with a specific grade point average or class ranking guaranteed admission to this college?

1343. If I graduate from a two-year college, am I guaranteed admission to this four-year college?

1344. What are the admissions requirements for home-schooled students?

1345. Will this college's admissions requirements be difficult for me?

1346. Will this college's admissions requirements be just right for me?

1347. Will this college's admissions requirements be very easy for me?

1348. Does this college provide pre-admissions counseling?

1349. Who can I ask about entrance requirements?

1350. What can I read about entrance requirements?

1351. What else should I know about entrance requirements at this college?

College Visits

1352. What colleges are in my local area?

1353. How do I make arrangements to visit colleges?

1354. Do I have to be invited or may I visit at any time?

1355. Do I need to make an appointment to visit, or can I just show up?

1356. Will I receive an itinerary, agenda or campus map prior to my visit?

1357. Are my parents and siblings welcome?

1358. What should I wear when I visit?

1359. Is there a campus dress code?

1360. When is the best time to visit? Fall? Spring? Summer?

1361. Are campus open houses scheduled on specific dates?

1362. Are special visits planned for gifted and talented students?

1363. Are special visits planned for athletes?

1364. Are special visits planned for scholarship students?

1365. Are special visits planned for honor students?

1366. Are special visits planned for any other groups of students?

1367. Are flexible visit times offered?

1368. Are weekend visits possible?

1369. Are overnight visits possible?

1370. Is overnight housing available on campus? Is there a fee?

1371. How do I make a reservation for overnight housing?

1372. How far in advance should I make my reservation?

1373. Can you recommend nearby hotels with discounted rates for visiting students?

1374. Will refreshments or meals be served during the visit?

1375. Can you recommend places to eat?

1376. Will a formal group presentation be made?

1377. Will a campus tour be conducted?

1378. Who conducts the official campus tours?

1379. Are video tours of the campus available for rent or purchase?

1380. Are campus tours available on the college Web site?

1381. Will I be able to talk with faculty?

1382. Will I be able to talk with administrators?

1383. Will I be able to talk to coaches?

1384. Will I be able to talk to students?

1385. Will I be able to talk to alumni?

1386. Should I get business cards from the people I meet?

1387. Will I be able to get a copy of the student newspaper?

1388. Will I be able to observe a class that is in session?

1389. Will I be able to eat in the cafeteria?

1390. Will I be able to visit the library?

1391. Will I be able to visit the bookstore?

1392. Do visiting students receive discounts on campus memorabilia?

1393. Will I be able to visit the residence halls or dormitories?

1394. Will I be able to tour the surrounding community?

1395. Where can I park during my visit?

1396. Is parking free for visitors?

1397. Is the parking lot within walking distance of the office hosting my visit?

1398. Is a free shuttle available?

1399. What will I do if it rains during my visit?

1400. Will someone contact me after I visit?

1401. Should I visit this college a second time before I accept an offer of admission?

1402. Who can I ask about college visits?

1403. What can I read about college visits?

1404. What else should I know about visiting this college?

Admissions Applications

1405. How many students apply to this college each year?

1406. What are the recruiting goals and priorities at this college?

1407. How do recruiters decide where they will go to recruit?

1408. Do I meet or fit the college's enrollment interests and needs?

1409. If this college contacts me first should I assume I will get admitted if I apply?

1410. How many colleges should I apply to?

1411. How do I decide which colleges I should apply to?

1412. Should I apply to colleges I like where I can easily get admitted?

1413. Should I apply to colleges I like where I have a good chance of being accepted?

1414. Should I apply to colleges I like that are a little out of my reach?

1415. What system should I use to organize my college applications?

1416. Should I start a file on each college contacted?

1417. Should I use a calendar to record all college-related deadlines, events and activities?

1418. Should I maintain a file summarizing all my activities and awards?

1419. Does this college require a pre-application?

1420. How do I obtain an application?

1421. Should I make a copy of the application and complete a rough draft of my information first?

1422. Is it possible to apply online?

1423. If an online application is completed will I still have to submit one on paper?

1424. Does this college accept any application forms other than its own?

1425. Are other application forms given the same consideration as this college's application?

1426. Is there an application fee?

1427. How much is the application fee?

1428. Can I pay the fee with a check? Money order? Credit card?

1429. Can the application fee be waived? Under what circumstances?

1430. When is the application deadline?

1431. Are more spots available if I apply early? How early?

1432. Is the application process the same for all applicants?

1433. Is the application deadline the same for all academic majors?

1434. Is there a supplemental application for certain academic majors?

1435. What kind of questions are asked on the application?

1436. Will I be asked about my background?

1437. Will I be asked about my parents' occupations, educational or socioeconomic level?

1438. Will I be asked if I am related to any alumni of this college?

1439. Will I be asked to list all the schools that I have attended?

1440. Will I be asked about my citizenship?

1441. Will I be asked about my employment history?

1442. Will I be asked about my volunteer experiences?

1443. Will I be asked about my residency classification?

1444. Will I be asked about my race or ethnicity?

1445. Will I be asked if English is a second language for me?

1446. Will I be asked why I am interested in this college?

1447. Will I be asked about my extra-curricular activities?

1448. Will I be asked about my employment history?

1449. Should I join lots of clubs in high school to make my application look impressive?

1450. Should I focus on participating in a few clubs in meaningful ways?

1451. Will I be asked about my educational goals?

1452. Will I be asked about my degree plans?

1453. Will I be asked about my intended major?

1454. Will I be asked if I have ever been charged with or subject to disciplinary action for misconduct?

1455. Will I be asked if I have ever been charged with a violation of the law that resulted in probation, community service or a jail sentence?

1456. Will I be asked if I have ever used recreational drugs?

1457. Will I be asked to provide emergency contact information?

1458. Should I answer questions about past behavior if my records have been expunged?

1459. Should my application be received by the deadline or postmarked by the deadline?

1460. Should I make a copy of the completed application for my files?

1461. How can I check the status of my application?

1462. Will I be notified that my application has been received?

1463. Where will my application be located? In the admissions office? My academic department? On the main campus? A branch campus?

1464. How long will my application remain on file?

1465. Can I reactivate my application?

1466. What makes an application distinctive?

1467. What are the most common mistakes applicants make?

1468. Should I hire a private college counselor to help with my college applications?

1469. What should I know about the private counselor's background and experience?

1470. What should I know about the private counselor's fees and services?

1471. Should I ask the private counselor for references?

1472. Who can I ask about college admissions?

1473. What can I read about college admissions?

1474. How can I contact the admissions office?

1475. Who is in charge of college admissions?

1476. Where is the admissions office located?

1477. When is the admissions office open? Evenings? Weekends?

1478. What else should I know about admissions applications?

Documents

Legal

1479. Which legal documents must be submitted with my application?

1480. Should I submit original documents or are copies acceptable?

1481. Will I need to provide my birth certificate?

1482. Will I need to provide proof of residency?

1483. Will I need to provide proof of citizenship?

1484. Will I need to provide a social security number?

1485. Will I need to provide a drivers license?

1486. Will I need to provide a vehicle registration?

1487. Will I need to provide a marriage certificate?

1488. Will I need to provide a voter registration card?

1489. Will I need to provide a copy of my military orders?

1490. Will I need to provide a resume?

1491. Who can I ask about the legal documents I need?

1492. What can I read about the legal documents I need?

1493. What else should I know about the legal documents I need to submit?

Transcripts

1494. Will I have to submit a high school transcript?

1495. How long does it take for my high school to send a transcript?

1496. Will I need to complete a transcript request form?

1497. Can my parents request my transcript?

1498. Can my high school transcripts be faxed, e-mailed, or hand-delivered?

1499. How will my transcript be evaluated?

1500. When do grades begin to count on my transcript?

1501. Will my high school grade point average be recalculated? How?

1502. Will grades in certain courses be weighted more heavily?

1503. Will I have to send a second transcript at a later time?

1504. Who can I ask about my transcript?

1505. What can I read about transcripts?

1506. What else should I know about transcripts?

Recommendation Letters

1507. Are recommendation letters required for admission?

1508. How many letters are required? May I

submit more than the required number?

1509. Am I required to submit letters from specific people, or can I choose?

1510. Must recommendation letters come from teachers in the academic major I plan to pursue?

1511. Is there a word or page limit for recommendation letters?

1512. Must a special form be submitted with my recommendation letter?

1513. How do I obtain any required recommendation forms?

1514. Can the recommendation form be downloaded from the college Web site?

1515. What types of questions are asked on the form?

1516. Will the recommender be asked to comment on my intellectual capabilities?

1517. Will the recommender be asked to

comment on my potential for academic growth?

1518. Will the recommender be asked to comment on my strengths and weaknesses?

1519. Will the recommender be asked to comment on my creativity?

1520. Will the recommender be asked to comment on my initiative?

1521. Will the recommender be asked to comment on my sensitivity to others?

1522. Will the recommender be asked to comment on my leadership potential?

1523. Will the recommender be asked to describe my talents?

1524. Will the recommender be asked to comment on my level of maturity?

1525. Will the recommender be asked to describe my personal achievements?

1526. Will the recommender be asked if I overcame any hardships?

1527. Will the recommender be asked if I have any significant work experience?

1528. Will the recommender be asked to compare me to other students at my high school?

1529. Will the recommender be asked how I chose my high school courses?

1530. How far ahead of time should my recommenders receive the information?

1531. Should I my recommenders receive copies of my academic records and a resume?

1532. Should I write a draft of my own recommendation and share it with my recommenders?

1533. Should recommendation letters be prepared on the recommender's letterhead?

1534. Should the recommendation letters be included with my application? Sent separately?

1535. Should I waive my access to review a recommendation letter?

1536. Should the recommendation letter be returned in a sealed envelope?

1537. When is the deadline for submitting recommendation letters?

1538. Can recommendation letters be faxed or e-mailed?

1539. Should I send my recommender a thank you note?

1540. Who can I ask about recommendation letters?

1541. What can I read about recommendation letters?

1542. What else should I know about recommendation letters?

Health Records

1543. Must I provide proof of immunization as a condition of enrollment?

1544. For which diseases must I show immunity?

1545. Must the shots have been received at a specific age or within a certain timeframe?

1546. How many vaccinations are required for each disease?

1547. What should I do if taking a vaccination is detrimental to my health?

1548. What should I do if taking a vaccination is against my religious beliefs?

1549. Do I have to complete an immunization form?

1550. Can my physician fax or e-mail proof of immunization?

1551. What if I know I had my shots but can't provide proof of immunization?

1552. Can I take a blood test?

1553. Will I be able to register for classes without proof of immunization?

1554. What is the deadline for submitting proof of immunizations?

1555. Who can I ask about my health records?

1556. What can I read about my health records?

1557. What else should I know about health records?

Essays

1558. Is an essay or personal statement required for admission?

1559. How important is the essay in the admissions process?

1560. Does this college provide an essay topic?

1561. What are some of the essay questions that have been asked in the past?

1562. Does the essay topic remain unchanged each year?

1563. Will I be asked to write about a significant personal experience?

1564. Will I be asked to write about an obstacle I have overcome?

1565. Will I be asked to write about a risk I took?

1566. Will I be asked to write about an ethical dilemma I faced and how I handled it?

1567. Will I be asked to write about a local, state, national or international issue?

1568. Will I be asked to describe my views about a political, social or historical issue?

1569. Will I be asked to write about a famous person who influenced me?

1570. Will I be asked why I chose to apply to this college?

1571. Will I be asked why I chose my intended major?

1572. Will I be asked to write on a topic of my choice?

1573. Should I get advice from other people on what to write about?

1574. Are there any word or page limitations?

1575. Which college official(s) will read my essay?

1576. What do readers look for in an essay?

1577. Will readers evaluate my writing skills in an essay?

1578. Will readers evaluate my opening or introductory statement?

1579. How should I start my essay?

1580. Should my essay begin with an attention grabbing statement?

1581. Should I start my essay with an interesting quote?

1582. Should my essay begin with a question?

1583. Will readers evaluate my spelling, grammar and punctuation?

1584. Will readers evaluate my vocabulary?

1585. Will readers look at how my paragraphs are developed?

1586. Will readers evaluate how I make transitions between paragraphs?

1587. Will readers look for specific examples to illustrate what I am writing about?

1588. Will readers pay attention to whether I use slang or cliches?

1589. Will readers pay attention to how my essay ends?

1590. How should I conclude my essay?

1591. Should the conclusion of my essay relate to the beginning?

1592. Should I read my essay out loud before I submit it?

1593. Should I have someone else read my essay for mistakes? Who?

1594. How many times should I expect to read and revise my essay?

1595. Should I hire an essay writing service to help me?

1596. What should I know about the essay writer's background and experience?

1597. What should I know about the service's fees?

1598. Should I ask the essay-writing service for references?

1599. Should I wait until I have all my documents before submitting my application for admission?

1600. How can I follow up to make sure my documents were received?

1601. Who can I ask about essays?

1602. What can I read about essays?

1603. What else should I know about submitting essays to this college?

Interviews

1604. How important is an interview in the admission process?

1605. Do I have to be invited for an interview by this college?

1606. Can I arrange an interview on my own?

1607. Should I visit the campus before scheduling an interview?

1608. Is an interview required for admission?

1609. How far in advance of the interview will I be notified?

1610. How many days do I have to be on campus?

1611. How many interviews will I have?

1612. Where will the interview be held?

1613. Will I have to do any written work during the interview process?

1614. Will my interview be one-on-one or with a group?

1615. What should I wear to the interview?

1616. What should I bring to the interview?

1617. Who will interview me?

1618. What questions will interviewers ask me?

1619. What are interviewers looking for?

1620. What is the interview procedure?

1621. What should I be prepared to discuss in the interview?

1622. Should I try to impress the interviewer by discussing everything I know about the college?

1623. Will the interviewer ask about my goals?

1624. Will the interviewer ask why I selected this college?

1625. Will the interviewer ask about my academic interests?

1626. Will the interviewer ask what inspired me to pursue my academic interests?

1627. Will the interviewer ask about my talents?

1628. Will the interviewer ask about my accomplishments?

1629. Will the interviewer ask about my hobbies?

1630. Will the interviewer ask what I like to read?

1631. Will the interviewer ask about people I admire or look up to?

1632. Will the interviewer ask how I spend my spare time?

1633. Will the interviewer ask about my strengths and weaknesses?

1634. Will the interviewer ask how I plan to overcome a weakness?

1635. What should I know about my body language during the interview?

1636. What questions should I ask the interviewer?

1637. Should my questions be tailored to my specific interests and intended major?

1638. What questions should I avoid asking the interviewer?

1639. What should I do when the interview is over?

1640. Should I get the interviewer's business card?

1641. Should I write a thank-you note?

1642. Who can I ask about interviews?

1643. What can I read about interviews?

1644. What else should I know about interviewing at this college?

Admissions

Decisions

1645. What does this college look for in an applicant?

1646. How are applications initially screened?

1647. Who does the initial screening?

1648. Who decides whether or not I am admitted? An individual? A committee?

1649. Who is the individual?

1650. Who serves on the committee?

1651. Are faculty members, alumni and/or students on the admissions committee?

1652. Are my grade point average and standardized exam score the only sources of information used to make decisions?

1653. What other information is used to make admissions decisions?

1654. Are special talents, community service, activities or leadership considered when making a decision?

1655. Are admissions and financial aid decisions made independently?

1656. Does my ability to pay tuition affect my admissions decision?

1657. What types of admissions decisions does this college make?

1658. Does this college make early decisions?

1659. Is it easier to get admitted if I apply as an early decision applicant?

1660. Will my application receive preferential treatment if I apply for early decision?

1661. If I apply for early decision will I receive special consideration for financial aid and merit scholarships?

1662. If I apply for early decision will this college provide an estimate of the financial aid I will receive? When?

1663. Does a favorable early decision obligate me to attend this college?

1664. Is there more than one early decision round?

1665. If I apply for early decision and I am not accepted will my application automatically be reviewed again in another decision group?

1666. Does this college take early action?

1667. Does a favorable early action decisions obligate me to attend this college?

1668. Does this college make rolling admissions or first-come, first-served decisions?

1669. Does this college have an open admissions policy?

1670. What is the deadline for each type of admissions decision?

1671. Does this college favor applications from particular types of high schools?

1672. How familiar is the admissions staff with my high school profile?

1673. How does this college view good grades and low test scores?

1674. How does this college view poor grades and high test scores?

1675. If my high school does not rank students will this lack of information hurt me in the admissions process?

1676. Is it a disadvantage if several people from the same high school apply to this college?

1677. Must this college admit a certain number of students from particular schools, communities, states, countries or academic majors?

1678. Do students who apply for the fall term admission receive preference over those who apply for the spring?

1679. Are my chances of being admitted greater in the spring or summer term?

1680. Does this college have a summer bridge program for first year students who want to enroll early?

1681. Does this college have late admits?

1682. What can I do to improve my chances of being accepted?

1683. Do I have an advantage if either of my parents graduated from this college?

1684. Do I have an advantage if either of my parents work at this college?

1685. Who can I ask about admissions decisions?

1686. What can I read about admissions decisions?

1687. What else do I need to know about admissions decisions at this college?

Acceptances

1688. How many students are admitted to this college?

1689. How many students who are offered and accept admission to this college actually enroll?

1690. When will I be notified of my admission status? How?

1691. Will I receive an acceptance letter? An e-mail? A phone call?

1692. Will my notification include intent-to-enroll information?

1693. Does this college make provisional admissions? Under what conditions?

1694. What happens if I am admitted and my final transcript shows that my grade point average has dropped?

1695. Will this college rescind its offer of admission if my final grade point average drops?

1696. Will my financial aid package be reduced if my final grade point average drops?

1697. When is the deadline for me to accept or decline an admission offer?

1698. If I accept this college's offer of admission will that prevent me from receiving offers from other colleges?

1699. Must I accept this offer before hearing from other colleges?

1700. Must I accept this offer before receiving a financial aid award letter?

1701. Will I be able to compare financial aid packages from different colleges before having to make a decision?

1702. Will I have to submit a tuition deposit upon accepting an offer?

1703. Will I have to submit a deposit if I am receiving financial aid?

1704. If I change my mind and decide to go elsewhere, will my admission deposit be refunded?

1705. If I change my mind, will I be required to obtain a written release from this college before I can attend elsewhere?

1706. Can my intent to enroll be faxed or e-mailed?

1707. Will my acceptance of admission be acknowledged or confirmed?

1708. When do I have to notify other colleges that I have decided to accept an offer?

1709. Will this college defer my admission if I want to wait a year before enrolling?

1710. May I defer admission to complete military service?

1711. If I wait a year, may I enroll in another college during that time?

1712. If I defer admission for a year, will I have to reapply?

1713. Will a "gap" in my schooling adversely affect my admission status?

1714. Who can I ask about accepting an admission offer?

1715. What can I read about accepting an admission offer?

1716. What else do I need to know about accepting admission to this college?

Rejections

1717. How many students are denied admission to this college?

1718. How many students reject this college's offer of admission?

1719. How many students are put on a wait list?

1720. What are my chances of gaining admission if I am wait listed?

1721. Of those on the wait list, how many are eventually admitted?

1722. What other options do I have if I am placed on a wait list?

1723. Should I write a follow-up letter to improve my chances of gaining admission?

1724. Will financial aid or residential housing be available by the time wait-listed students are notified?

1725. How long will I remain on the wait list before being notified that I will not be admitted?

1726. If I am on the waiting list and am not accepted can I reapply for the next term?

1727. What other options are available if I am not accepted?

1728. Can I appeal my admissions decision? How? To whom?

1729. If I am not accepted can I attend another college now and reapply to this college later as a transfer student?

1730. Who can I ask about admissions rejections?

1731. What can I read about admissions rejections?

1732. What else do I need to know about admissions rejections at this college?

Financial Assistance

College Costs

1733. How much does it cost to attend this college?

1734. How are tuition costs computed? By credit hour? Term? Year of study?

1735. How much is per-credit-hour tuition?

1736. How much is undergraduate in-state tuition?

1737. How much is graduate in-state tuition?

1738. How much is undergraduate out-of-state tuition?

1739. How much is graduate-out-of-state tuition?

1740. How much of the total cost is for full-time tuition? Part-time tuition?

1741. How much of the total cost is for books and supplies?

1742. How much is for room and board?

1743. How much is for transportation costs?

1744. How much is for personal expenses?

1745. How much is for other expenses?

1746. What is included in "other" expenses?

1747. Are private lessons included in other expenses?

1748. Is a private room included in other expenses?

1749. Are course overloads included in other expenses?

1750. How much will it cost if I live on campus? Off campus?

1751. When was the last time tuition increased at this college? How much?

1752. Is tuition expected to increase in the next four to six years? How much?

1753. Who can I ask about college costs?

1754. What can I read about college costs?

1755. What else should I know about how much it costs to attend this college?

Kinds of Assistance

Loans

1756. How many students at this college receive loans?

1757. Does this college provide a list of private student loan lenders?

1758. Does this college offer subsidized loans? Unsubsidized loans?

1759. Will I be required to provide security for this loan?

1760. What is the maximum amount I can borrow?

1761. Must I borrow the full amount? Can I ask for less?

1762. When do I have to pay the loan back?

1763. Can I receive more than one loan?

1764. Does this college make loans to parents?

1765. How much can my parents borrow?

1766. Can my parents apply for more than one loan?

1767. What are the current loan interest rates?

1768. Do I have to pay any other charges or fees to obtain a loan?

1769. What is the procedure for applying for a loan?

1770. Is the procedure the same if I am financially independent?

1771. Does this college make short-term loans?

1772. Must I sign a promissory note?

1773. What is this college's loan default rate?

1774. What are my rights and responsibilities as a borrower?

1775. Who can I ask about college loans?

1776. What can I read about college loans?

1777. What else should I know about loans at this college?

Grants

1778. Does this college award grants?

1779. How many students receive grants?

1780. What is the size of the average grant award?

1781. Does this college provide a list of grant providers?

1782. Can I receive more than one grant?

1783. What is the procedure for applying for grants?

1784. Under which circumstances must grants be paid back?

1785. Who can I ask about grant awards?

1786. What can I read about grant awards?

1787. What else should I know about grant awards at this college?

Employment

1788. Does this college award work-study jobs?

1789. How many students work while they study at this college?

1790. What is the procedure for applying for work-study jobs?

1791. How do I find a work-study job?

1792. Are on-campus jobs readily available or hard to find?

1793. Where are the best places to work on campus?

1794. Can I use my work-study award to work off campus?

1795. Will my work-study award allow me to work as much as I want?

1796. Will I have to maintain and submit a time sheet or time card?

1797. Will I be able to study during my work hours?

1798. How much will I be paid?

1799. Will I be paid minimum wage?

1800. Can I be paid more than minimum wage depending on the work I do?

1801. Will I be paid by the hour? By salary? By commission?

1802. How frequently will I be paid? Weekly? Biweekly? Monthly?

1803. Will I receive a paycheck?

1804. Will Social Security and income taxes be deducted from my paycheck?

1805. Will I be required to direct deposit my paycheck?

1806. Can I earn more than the amount of work-study money that I am awarded?

1807. Will I be paid for lunch, sick days, vacation days or official holidays?

1808. Who can I ask about work-study jobs?

1809. What can I read about work-study jobs?

1810. What else should I know about work-study jobs at this college?

Scholarships and Prizes

1811. Does this college award scholarships?

1812. Where does this college's scholarship money come from?

1813. How many students receive scholarships to attend this college?

1814. Which scholarships do students receive during their first year, sophomore, junior or senior year in college?

1815. How can I obtain a list of scholarships awarded by this college?

1816. What are the criteria for receiving a scholarship?

1817. What is the application process for scholarships?

1818. Can I receive more than one scholarship?

1819. Does this college award prizes?

1820. Where does this college's prize money come from?

1821. How much can I win in prize money?

1822. How can I obtain a list of prizes?

1823. How often are prizes awarded?

1824. Should I pay a scholarship search service?

1825. How much does this service cost?

1826. How will I know the scholarship service is credible?

1827. Who can I ask about scholarships and prizes?

1828. What can I read about scholarships and prizes?

1829. What else should I know about scholarships or prizes at this college?

Sources of Assistance

Savings and Investments

1830. How soon should I begin to save for college?

1831. How much money should I have saved to attend this college?

1832. Where should I save my money?

1833. Should I put money in a savings account?

1834. Should I put money in a certificate of deposit?

1835. Should I put money in a money market account?

1836. Should I put money in a savings bond?

1837. Should I invest money in a mutual fund?

1838. Should I invest money in stocks and bonds?

1839. Should I invest money in treasury bills, notes or bonds?

1840. Should I invest money in insurance policies?

1841. Should I invest money in an individual retirement account for education?

1842. Should I invest money in a prepaid tuition plan?

1843. Can I withdraw money from my savings or investments at any time without penalty?

1844. Can I borrow against the cash value of insurance policies?

1845. Can I borrow against the appraised value of real estate?

1846. Will I lose money if I withdraw my money sooner than I planned?

1847. Does this college accept a prepaid tuition savings plan? Which one(s)?

1848. How many students are on a prepaid tuition plan?

1849. What does the prepaid tuition plan cover? Tuition? Fees? Room and board?

1850. What are the current interest rates on savings accounts?

1851. What are the current rates of return on investments?

1852. Will my family be penalized for saving for college?

1853. Who can I ask about savings and investments?

1854. What can I read about savings and investments?

1855. What else should I know about saving and investing to attend this college?

Federal Aid

1856. Does this college participate in all federal student aid programs?

1857. How many students at this college receive federal financial aid?

1858. What does federal financial aid cover?

1859. Is federal aid need-based? Merit-based?

1860. What is the procedure for applying for federal financial aid?

1861. When is the deadline to apply for federal financial aid?

1862. How will the federal government know I want to attend this college?

1863. Will my family have the same expenses regardless of the college I select?

1864. How will this college be notified that I have been awarded federal financial aid?

1865. What are the tax implications of receiving financial aid?

1866. Am I required to report financial aid as taxable income on my tax return?

1867. What are the federal tax benefits associated with receiving financial aid?

1868. What are the federal tax penalties associated with receiving financial aid?

1869. If I file for government tax credits will my expected family contribution increase?

1870. Who can I ask about federal financial aid?

1871. What can I read about federal financial aid?

1872. What else should I know about federally-funded financial aid at this college?

State Aid

1873. Does this college participate in state-funded financial aid programs?

1874. How many students receive state aid?

1875. What type of state aid is available? Grants? Loans? Scholarships?

1876. Where can I get a list of state-funded financial aid resources?

1877. What is the procedure for applying for state aid?

1878. When is the deadline to apply for state financial aid?

1879. Do I have to be a resident of this college's state to receive state aid?

1880. What is required to prove I am eligible for state aid?

1881. If my parents reside in different states, can I claim residency in either state?

1882. Who can I ask about state aid?

1883. What can I read about state aid?

1884. What else should I know about state-funded financial aid at this college?

Institutional Aid

1885. Does this college use any of its own funds to provide financial assistance?

1886. How many students receive institutional aid?

1887. Where can I get a list of available institutional aid offered?

1888. What types of institutional aid does this college provide?

1889. What is the procedure for applying for institutional aid?

1890. When is the deadline to apply for institutional aid?

1891. Does each academic department have its own funds for financial assistance?

1892. How many students in my intended major received departmental aid?

1893. What type of assistance does my academic department provide?

1894. Does my academic department award grants?

1895. Does my academic department award scholarships?

1896. Does my academic department award tuition waivers?

1897. If my parents or relatives work for this college will my tuition be waived?

1898. If I work for this college full time will my tuition be waived?

1899. If I work for a federal, state or local government agency will my tuition be waived?

1900. If I work as a teaching or research assistant, will my tuition be waived?

1901. If I have a special talent that this college is seeking, will my tuition be waived?

1902. If I am an athlete, will my tuition be waived?

1903. If I am a senior citizen, will my tuition be waived?

1904. How many students in my intended major receive departmental aid?

1905. What is the procedure for applying for departmental aid?

1906. When is the deadline to apply for departmental financial aid?

1907. Who can I ask about institutional aid?

1908. What can I read about institutional aid?

1909. What else should I know about institutional aid at this college?

Private Aid

1910. Where can I find sources of private financial aid?

1911. How early should I start looking for scholarships?

1912. Does this college have a list of scholarships or prizes students earn by entering national, state or local academic contests?

1913. Which local community groups and organizations award scholarships?

1914. Which corporations award scholarships?

1915. Which private businesses award scholarships?

1916. Which individuals award scholarships?

1917. Have prior students received aid from labor unions?

1918. Have prior students received aid from civic groups?

1919. Have prior students received aid from professional associations?

1920. Have prior students received aid from foundations?

1921. Have prior students received aid from religious organizations?

1922. Have prior students received aid from the armed forces?

1923. Is a list of private aid sources received by students at this college available?

1924. If I receive private aid, do I have to report it to the college?

1925. Can my employer pay my tuition?

1926. Will I have to pay my tuition and then have my employer reimburse me?

1927. Who can I talk to about scholarships?

1928. What do you recommend I read to learn more about scholarships?

1929. Who can I ask about private financial aid?

1930. What can I read about private financial aid?

1931. What else should I know about private financial aid at this college?

Eligibility

1932. How many students at this college receive financial aid?

1933. Do I have to be a United States citizen to receive aid?

1934. Am I eligible for aid if I am a permanent resident?

1935. Is a high school diploma or its equivalent required to be eligible?

1936. Do I have to be in a certain income bracket to be eligible for aid?

1937. Is a certain grade point average required to be eligible for aid?

1938. Are certain test scores required to be eligible for aid?

1939. Do I have to be degree-seeking to be eligible for aid?

1940. Do I have to be enrolled full time to be eligible for aid?

1941. Do I have to be enrolled part time to be eligible for aid?

1942. Do I have to be an undergraduate student to be eligible for aid?

1943. Do I have to be a graduate student to be eligible for aid?

1944. Do I have to declare a certain major to be eligible for aid?

1945. Do I have to be independent to be eligible for aid?

1946. Do I have to dependent on someone else to be eligible for aid?

1947. Do I have to be drug free to be eligible?

1948. Am I eligible for aid if I have been incarcerated?

1949. Am I eligible for aid if I have been convicted of the sale or possession of illegal drugs?

1950. Do I have to be registered with the selective service to be eligible?

1951. If I am enrolled in two colleges am I eligible to receive aid from both colleges?

1952. Am I eligible for aid if I am in default on a student loan at another college?

1953. Am I eligible to deduct educational expenses on my federal tax return?

1954. Who can I ask to determine my eligibility for financial aid?

1955. What can I read about eligibility for financial aid?

1956. What else do I need to know about eligibility for financial aid at this college?

Financial Aid Applications

1957. How many students apply for financial aid?

1958. What is the procedure for applying for financial aid?

1959. Which financial aid application form(s) must be completed?

1960. Is there a separate application form for federal aid?

1961. Is there a separate application form for state aid?

1962. Is there a separate application form for local aid?

1963. Is there a separate application form for institutional aid?

1964. Where can I obtain an application form?

1965. Does this college offer free help to complete my forms?

1966. Should I hire a financial consultant to help me apply for financial aid?

1967. What should I know about the consultant's background and experience?

1968. What should I know about the consultant's fees and services?

1969. Should I ask the consultant for references?

1970. What other documents are needed to complete the application?

1971. Will I need to provide proof of income?

1972. Will I need to submit my parents' tax returns?

1973. How early should my parents file their tax returns in my senior year?

1974. Does the application process differ if my parents are divorced?

1975. Does the application process differ if my parents don't work or have lost their jobs?

1976. Can I apply for financial aid online?

1977. Is there an application fee?

1978. When is the application deadline?

1979. Will I be notified that my application was received?

1980. Will I be notified if any information is missing?

1981. Will the accuracy of the information I submit be verified?

1982. Am I required to apply for government aid before I can be awarded institutional or private aid?

1983. Does this college's financial aid application deadline precede governmental deadlines?

1984. What happens after I apply for financial aid?

1985. What if I originally applied for financial aid at a different college and now I want to attend your college?

1986. What are the most common mistakes people make when applying for financial aid?

1987. Should I apply even if I think I am ineligible for aid?

1988. Can I make corrections to my application?

1989. Who can I ask about applying for financial aid?

1990. What can I read about applying for financial aid?

1991. Who is in charge of the financial aid office?

1992. How can I contact current students

who are on financial aid?

1993. Where is the financial aid office located?

1994. When is the financial aid office open? Evenings? Weekends?

1995. What else should I know about applying for financial aid?

Decisions

1996. How is financial need determined?

1997. Is a formula used to calculate how my family will be expected to pay?

1998. Does the formula take into consideration the cost of attending this college?

1999. What does a typical financial aid award package include?

2000. If I apply to more than one college, will my award packages vary?

2001. How often does financial aid cover the full cost of attending this college?

2002. Are my family's income and expenses taken into consideration?

2003. Are my family's assets taken into consideration?

2004. Which is more important when determining aid, income or assets?

2005. When will I be notified of a financial aid decision?

2006. How much financial aid am I eligible to receive?

2007. How much will I be awarded?

2008. Will my award cover each year of attendance?

2009. Does the award have a time limit?

2010. Does this college engage in award negotiation?

2011. Can the deadline for accepting my award package be extended if I'm negotiating changes?

2012. Is there a limit on how much aid I can receive each year?

2013. If I change schools will my aid automatically go with me?

2014. Will additional scholarships reduce the amount of financial aid I can receive?

2015. If I receive a scholarship after accepting my financial aid award do I have to report it?

2016. Will my award package be adjusted based on any additional scholarships?

2017. If my family's financial circumstances change can I ask for more aid?

2018. How much time do I have to use my financial aid?

2019. What if the financial aid I receive does not cover all my expenses?

2020. Who decides how much aid I will receive? An individual? A committee? A computer?

2021. Who is the individual?

2022. Who serves on the committee?

2023. Can I appeal my financial aid decision? To whom? How?

2024. Who can I talk to about my financial aid decision?

2025. What can I read about my financial aid decision?

2026. What else do I need to know about financial aid decisions?

Disbursements

2027. How will I receive my loans, grants, scholarships or other financial aid?

2028. Will the money come to me directly?

2029. Will the money go to my parents?

2030. Will the money automatically go toward my term bill?

2031. How will I be notified that my funds have arrived at this college?

2032. How frequently will aid money come to me or this college?

2033. Will I receive the full award all at once?

2034. Will the funds be received in installments?

2035. How often will installment payments be made? Each term? Each year?

2036. Will I receive the same amount each year?

2037. Will the amount increase? Decrease? Under what circumstances?

2038. If any money is left after paying my tuition and fees, can it be spent on whatever I want?

2039. Who can I talk to about financial aid disbursements?

2040. What can I read about financial aid disbursements?

2041. Who is in charge of disbursing financial aid?

2042. What else should I know about how financial aid is disbursed at this college?

Renewal

2043. Do I need to reapply for financial aid every year?

2044. Is the reapplication process the same for scholarships, grants, loans and work-study jobs?

2045. Will I be notified when it is time to reapply or will I have to remember?

2046. How will I be notified? By E-mail? Snail mail?

2047. When will I be notified? At the end of each academic year?

2048. Will I have to start all over, or can I just update my application?

2049. What can prevent me from receiving aid in the future?

2050. Does failure to make satisfactory academic progress affect future financial aid?

2051. Which grade point average is used to determine satisfactory academic progress? My term grade point average? My overall grade point average?

2052. Who can I talk to about renewing my financial aid?

2053. What can I read about renewing my financial aid?

2054. Who is in charge of renewing financial aid?

2055. What else should I know about renewing financial aid at this college?

Repayment

2056. What is the total amount of money I will have to repay?

2057. When will I have to pay back my loans?

2058. Will I have to pay my loans back when I drop below full-time status?

2059. Will I have to pay my loans back if I don't enroll for a calendar year?

2060. Will I have to pay my loans back when I withdraw from this college?

2061. Will I have to pay my loans back when I graduate?

2062. Is there a grace period before I must begin repayment? How long is the grace period?

2063. What are the repayment terms of my loans?

2064. Will I receive a loan repayment schedule? When?

2065. How much will I have to pay each month?

2066. Will I have to pay a fixed monthly amount?

2067. Will monthly payments gradually increase as my income increases?

2068. Will I receive a monthly billing statement?

2069. Can my payments be automatically deducted from my bank account each month?

2070. What is the interest rate on my loan?

2071. Is the interest rate fixed or variable?

2072. Can I refinance my loan to secure a lower interest rate?

2073. Will interest only be paid for a certain period of time?

2074. Can all my loans be consolidated so I only make one monthly payment?

2075. Does this college have a reduced payment plan?

2076. Can loan payments be deferred? How many times?

2077. Can I postpone repayment through a forbearance agreement? How many times?

2078. Can loan payments be deferred if I am enrolled in a fulltime internship or residency program that is required for licensure, registration or certification?

2079. Can loan payments be deferred if I am pursuing a course of study in an approved graduate fellowship program?

2080. Can loan payments be deferred if I am in an approved rehabilitation training program for the disabled?

2081. Can loan payments be deferred if I am on active duty in the military?

2082. Can loan payments be deferred if I experience an economic hardship?

2083. Can loan payments be deferred if I am unemployed and unable to secure employment?

2084. Will interest continue to accrue during the deferment period?

2085. Can a portion of my loans be cancelled if I work in certain professions?

2086. Can a portion of my loans be cancelled if I am a full-time volunteer in an approved tax-exempt organization?

2087. Will my loan be cancelled if this college closes?

2088. Will my loan be cancelled if I become totally and permanently disabled?

2089. Is a forbearance or deferment given automatically?

2090. Which forms must be completed to request a postponement, deferment or cancellation of all my loans?

2091. May I pre-pay all or part of my loan at any time without penalty?

2092. What happens if I become delinquent on my loan?

2093. Must I pay a late charge if payment is not made on time? How much?

2094. Will my payment history be reported to a credit bureau?

2095. Do I have to repay the loan if I am not gainfully employed?

2096. Who is responsible for repaying a loan given to my parents? Me or my parents?

2097. When do my parents have to begin paying their loan back?

2098. What happens if I default on paying back a loan?

2099. Will defaulted funds be unavailable to other students?

2100. Can my lender take legal action if I default on a loan?

2101. Will I lose eligibility for future government student aid if I default on a loan?

2102. Will I jeopardize my government income tax refund if I default on a loan?

2103. What is this college's loan default rate?

2104. Who can I ask about repaying my financial aid?

2105. What can I read about repaying financial aid?

2106. Who is in charge of collecting loan payments?

2107. What else should I know about repaying financial aid?

Living on Campus

2108. How many students live on campus?

2109. Am I required to live on campus?

2110. Am I required to live within a certain-mile radius to be exempt from a residency requirement?

2111. Are certain groups of students required to live on campus? Freshmen? Athletes? Honor students? International students?

2112. What is the procedure for applying for on-campus housing?

2113. Is there a housing application fee?

2114. Is the housing application procedure the same if I am married and have a family?

2115. Can I apply for housing online?

2116. When is the deadline for applying for housing?

2117. How much does it cost to live on campus?

2118. What is included in my housing fee?

2119. Do housing fees cover telephone service?

2120. Do housing fees cover Internet access?

2121. What specifications must my computer have to be compatible with the housing network?

2122. Do housing fees cover cable television?

2123. Are some housing facilities less expensive than others? Why?

2124. Is on-campus housing reasonably priced compared to living off campus?

2125. How often do room rates increase?

2126. When was the last time room rates increased? By how much?

2127. Will I have to make a housing deposit?

2128. Is my housing deposit refundable?

2129. How long does it take to receive a refund?

2130. Do I have to sign a housing contract?

2131. Can I cancel or be released from my housing contract?

2132. Can I sublease a housing contract?

2133. Am I guaranteed housing until I graduate?

2134. Do I have to reapply for housing each year?

2135. Can I transfer to another residence hall? How?

2136. Will I be required to move to another residence hall after earning a certain number of credit hours?

2137. Will I be required to move off campus after earning a certain number of credit hours?

2138. How close is housing to the classrooms?

2139. Are residence halls spread throughout campus? Clustered?

2140. What year was the hall I may be living in built?

2141. What is the designated capacity of the residence halls?

2142. What is the current housing occupancy rate? Full? Empty?

2143. How many floors are in each building?

2144. Is there an elevator in each building?

2145. Is housing accessible to the disabled?

2146. Are the residence halls noisy or quiet?

2147. Are certain residence halls organized by student groups, characteristics or themes?

2148. What are the different types of building designs and floor plans?

2149. Are floor plans designed as dorms, apartments, or cooperative housing?

2150. Will I have to share a bathroom with others who live in my room?

2151. Will I have to share a bathroom with others who live on my hall floor?

2152. Are single rooms available if I don't want to share a room?

2153. Is there a study area in my room? In the building?

2154. Is there a kitchen in my room? In the building?

2155. Do I have to bring kitchen utensils?

2156. Is a computer lab located in the building?

2157. Are all rooms air-conditioned? Heated?

2158. Will I be able to control the thermostat, or is the temperature control centralized?

2159. At what temperature is the centralized air or heat maintained?

2160. Can I have an air conditioner installed?

2161. Can I bring a fan or space heater into my room?

2162. Are there washing machines and dryers in each room? In the building? On each floor?

2163. Are laundry facilities provided in close proximity to living areas?

2164. Are the laundry machines free, swipe-card or coin operated?

2165. Is there an exercise room in the building?

2166. Is there a television or game room in the building?

2167. Is storage or locker space available in the building?

2168. Is storage space available in close proximity?

2169. What furnishings are provided in each unit?

2170. What personal furnishings and equipment should I bring?

2171. May I have a refrigerator in my room? What size?

2172. Can I bring cooking appliances? Which ones?

2173. Do I need to bring linens and towels?

2174. What size bed sheets should I bring?

2175. Do I need to bring a lamp? What is the maximum wattage?

2176. Do I need to bring an iron and ironing board?

2177. Do I need to bring a vacuum cleaner?

2178. Do I need to bring cleaning supplies?

2179. Can I move college furniture out of my room and replace it with my own?

2180. Can I move college furniture out of a lounge and bring it into my room?

2181. How often are furnishings, carpets or window treatments replaced?

2182. How often are the rooms and building painted?

2183. How often are the community bathrooms and other public areas cleaned?

2184. Am I expected to clean the kitchen, bathrooms and public areas?

2185. Who supervises the students who live in residence halls?

2186. Do faculty members reside in the residence halls?

2187. Do residence halls have resident assistants?

2188. What is the role of a resident assistant?

2189. Do current students serve as resident assistants?

2190. What type of security is provided in the residence halls?

2191. Is there a curfew for housing residents?

2192. Do resident assistants conduct "room checks?" How often?

2193. Are residence halls co-ed? Female only? Male only?

2194. Are men and women separated by floors? Alternate rooms? Wings?

2195. Are members of the opposite sex allowed to visit my room?

2196. When are visiting hours for the opposite sex?

2197. Can I have a guest stay in my room overnight?

2198. Do I need the consent of my

roommates to host an overnight guest?

2199. Is smoking, drug use or alcohol consumption allowed in residence halls?

2200. Are weapons or firearms permitted in residence halls?

2201. Are animals, birds or reptiles permitted in residence halls?

2202. Is there a separate disciplinary code for students who live in on-campus housing?

2203. Will I have to move out of housing if I violate the housing code?

2204. Does the general public have access to meeting rooms or other facilities in the residence halls?

2205. Can I operate a business in the residence hall?

2206. When will I be notified that I have been approved for housing?

2207. How are room and roommate assignments made?

2208. Are there quiet study floors?

2209. Are there floors for upper classmen?

2210. Are there chemically-sensitive floors?

2211. May I see my room before I move in?

2212. When can I move in?

2213. What will my new address be?

2214. How will I receive mail?

2215. Can I ship my personal belongings to campus before my arrival?

2216. Where will my belongings be stored until I arrive?

2217. How will I receive my room key?

2218. Will I have to leave a key deposit?

2219. What happens if I lose my key?

2220. What do housing residents do when they are not studying?

2221. Are certain activities restricted only to housing residents?

2222. How is a residence hall governed?

2223. Is there a hall or resident student council? Club? Committee?

2224. How can I get involved with hall organizations?

2225. How often am I expected to go home?

2226. When do the residence halls close for holiday or vacation breaks?

2227. Can I stay in my room during breaks?

2228. Can I leave my belongings in my room during school breaks?

2229. How safe are my possessions if I am going home during the break?

2230. Is loss, damage, or theft of my personal property covered under this college's insurance policy?

2231. Should I insure my personal property?

2232. What is the residence hall evacuation policy and procedure?

2233. What is the residence hall fire drill policy and procedure?

2234. What forms of security are in place around the residence halls?

2235. Is housing leased by this college or provided by a third party?

2236. When can I move off campus?

2237. What are the advantages and disadvantages of living on campus?

2238. What are the most common mistakes students make on a housing application?

2239. Who can I ask about living on campus?

2240. What can I read about living on campus?

2241. Who is in charge of residential housing?

2242. How can I contact current residential students?

2243. How can I contact the residential housing office?

2244. Where is the residential housing office located?

2245. When is the residential housing office open? Evenings? Weekends?

2246. What else should I know about living on campus?

Eating on Campus

2247. What is the quality of food on campus?

2248. What is the quality of drinking water on campus?

2249. What kind of dining facilities are available on campus?

2250. What kind of dining options are available? Hot food? Fast food?

2251. Who prepares and serves the food? College students? College employees?

2252. Does this college have a contract with a food service company to prepare and serve food?

2253. Which outside contractor provides the food service?

2254. How much variety do students have at each meal?

2255. What if I have special dietary needs?

2256. Does the dining hall prepare kosher, low-salt and/or vegetarian dishes?

2257. Am I required to purchase a meal plan?

2258. What is the most popular meal plan? Why?

2259. Does the meal plan include breakfast, lunch and dinner?

2260. Does the meal plan provide a buffet service?

2261. Does the meal plan provide a la carte service?

2262. How large are the a la carte portions?

2263. Is the meal plan offered seven days per week? Six days? Five days?

2264. Where can my meal plan be used on campus? At the student union? In the residence halls? At a snack bar?

2265. Do the hours vary at the different locations?

2266. Do meal hours vary from one location to another?

2267. Are food services provided beyond regularly scheduled mealtimes?

2268. Are menus and prices posted at each location?

2269. Does the meal plan require me to eat within a specific timeframe?

2270. Will I be required to eat my meals with other students?

2271. Will I be required to follow a certain dress code at mealtime?

2272. How do I sign up for the meal plan?

2273. Can I change my meal plan?

2274. How will my meals be paid for at the cash register?

2275. Can I invite a guest to meals?

2276. Can my meals be shared with a guest?

2277. How much does it cost for a guest to eat with me?

2278. Will I have to deposit money on a swipe card to pay for meals?

2279. Will a separate identification card be issued for my meal plan?

2280. What happens if my meal card is lost?

2281. What are the advantages and disadvantages of eating on campus?

2282. Who can I ask about eating on campus?

2283. What can I read about eating on campus?

2284. Who is in charge of food services?

2285. How can I contact the food services office?

2286. Where is the food service office located?

2287. When is the food services office open? Evenings? Weekends?

2288. What else should I know about eating on campus at this college?

Living off Campus

2289. How many students live off campus?

2290. How many live in Greek organization, or fraternity and sorority houses?

2291. What are the advantages and disadvantages of living in Greek housing?

2292. Does it cost more to live in Greek housing?

2293. Does it cost more to eat in Greek housing?

2294. How do I apply to live in Greek housing?

2295. Do I have to join a fraternity or sorority to reside in Greek housing?

2296. What is the procedure for joining?

2297. Are first year students permitted to become members of fraternities and sororities?

2298. Do I have to pledge or make a commitment to a particular fraternity or sorority?

2299. How long is the pledge period?

2300. What will I be asked to do during the pledge period?

2301. Is hazing permitted at this college?

2302. What is this college's hazing policy?

2303. What are the consequences if the hazing policy is violated?

2304. How many students at this college have been killed or injured as a result of hazing?

2305. How will my social life differ if I live in Greek housing?

2306. Will most of my free time be spent with other members?

2307. Will I have to perform house chores and maintenance duties?

2308. Will I be expected to attend Greek parties and events?

2309. Are first year students allowed to attend fraternity and sorority sponsored events?

2310. How many students live in rented rooms, apartments or houses?

2311. Will someone at this college help me find off-campus housing?

2312. Is there a real estate company on campus to assist with off-campus housing?

2313. How can I find out which rooms, houses and apartments are available for rent?

2314. Is there a host family program at this college?

2315. How expensive is it to live off campus?

2316. How much should I expect to pay to rent an apartment?

2317. How much should I expect to pay for an efficiency apartment?

2318. How much should I expect to pay to share a room?

2319. Are apartments, efficiencies or rooms furnished? Unfurnished?

2320. If I share a room will I have access to a kitchen?

2321. Will I be able to cook in the kitchen? In my room?

2322. Do I need to have my own cooking utensils?

2323. Will my rent also cover utilities?

2324. Will utility bill accounts be established in my name or the landlord's name?

2325. Will my rent cover maintenance and repair costs?

2326. Who will be responsible for making the repairs? Me? The landlord?

2327. Should I get to know my neighbors?

2328. Should I purchase renters insurance?

2329. Will I have to pay a security deposit?

2330. Will someone at this college review a lease agreement for me?

2331. Can I sublease if I change my mind about wanting to live off campus?

2332. Is there a moving company on campus?

2333. Will someone at this college assist me with a landlord dispute?

2334. How many students commute to campus?

2335. How do commuter students travel back and forth to campus?

2336. How much time will it take to get to campus from where I live off campus?

2337. How many hours per week will my commute require?

2338. Does this college publish a commuter student directory?

2339. Is a share-a-ride board available on campus? Where?

2340. Is there a carpooling program on campus?

2341. What happens if I miss class because a carpool driver has mechanical problems?

2342. Where will I be able to park when I arrive on campus?

2343. Are commuter students represented in student government?

2344. Is there a commuter student club or organization on campus?

2345. Is there a place on campus where commuter students gather between classes?

2346. Are activities and events scheduled at times when commuter students can participate?

2347. What are the advantages and disadvantages of living off campus?

2348. Who can I ask about living off campus?

2349. What can I read about living off campus?

2350. Who is in charge of commuter student services?

2351. How can I contact current commuter students?

2352. How can I contact the commuter student office?

2353. Where is the commuter student office located?

2354. When is the commuter student office open? Evenings? Weekends?

2355. What else should I know about living off campus?

FAQ's About Staying In College

PART II

"There is no such thing as a stupid question."

Anonymous

Think of this phase of the college experience as a time to assemble the inside of the puzzle. Each attempt to connect one puzzle piece to another is an experience of trial and error. The topics in this section will help reduce the number of errors you make. Begin by working on the "pile" of orientation questions first, as they will be central to connecting the adjoining pieces of your puzzle.

As you move through each pile, notice how each piece differs. Don't get frustrated if pieces are missing. They may turn up later. And be sure to ask for help if you need it.

The key to putting the inside of your college puzzle together is to think of yourself as a 'knob' and 'socket'-shaped piece. Sometimes you will need to stick your neck out, and sometimes you will need to be receptive to new people and ideas. But never lose sight of the big picture.

Orientation

2356. How is this college's orientation provided to new students?

2357. Is orientation a one- or two-day program?

2358. Is orientation a non-credit course?

2359. Is orientation a credit course?

2360. Is attendance at orientation required or optional?

2361. Can I participate in orientation online?

2362. When is orientation scheduled?

2363. When will I be notified of orientation? How?

2364. Do I have to register in advance?

2365. Is there an orientation fee? How much?

2366. Is there a separate orientation for students in my intended major?

2367. Is there a separate orientation for international students?

2368. Is there a separate orientation for multicultural students?

2369. Is there a separate orientation for student athletes?

2370. Is there a separate orientation for transfer students?

2371. Is there a separate orientation for parents and family members?

2372. When should I arrive on campus?

2373. What kind of clothes should I wear during orientation?

2374. What activities are scheduled during orientation?

2375. Are campus tours scheduled?

2376. Are luncheons, picnics or dinners scheduled?

2377. Are parties or dances scheduled?

2378. Are presentations by the president or other administrators scheduled?

2379. Are presentations by the dean or faculty scheduled?

2380. Are presentations by student support services scheduled?

2381. Are presentations by academic support services scheduled?

2382. Are parent socials scheduled?

2383. Will early advising for my first term be available?

2384. Will early registration for my first term be available?

2385. What should I bring to orientation?

2386. Should I bring my file of all the correspondence I received from the college?

2387. Should I bring a valid photo identification card?

2388. Should I bring an organizer with a calendar?

2389. Will I get a college identification card (ID)?

2390. Will I have my photograph taken?

2391. When will I receive my ID card?

2392. Will I have to pick my ID card up at a later date or time?

2393. Will my ID card be mailed to me?

2394. Where can I use my ID card?

2395. When will I be required to use my ID card?

2396. Is my ID also my library borrower card?

2397. Is my ID card needed to gain access to campus buildings?

2398. Does my ID card also function as my dining card?

2399. Does my ID card also function as a calling card?

2400. Does my ID card also function as a debit card?

2401. If I run out of money can cash be added to my ID card?

2402. Will my ID card enable me to gain access to student events free of charge?

2403. How often do I need to get a new ID card?

2404. What if my ID card is lost or stolen?

2405. What if my ID gets bent, broken or demagnetizes?

2406. Can I get a temporary ID card?

2407. Can I have more than one ID card?

2408. Will I have to relinquish my ID card when I leave this college?

2409. Will I have to take any tests to be assigned the proper classes?

2410. Can I register for classes before placement tests are taken?

2411. Which placement tests will I have to take? English? Math? Reading?

2412. How can I prepare for placement tests?

2413. Are practice tests available?

2414. How much time is allotted for each placement test?

2415. What should I bring to the test? Pencils? A calculator?

2416. Can my placement tests be taken online?

2417. Can I fail placement tests?

2418. What happens if I score low on a placement test?

2419. What if I feel my test results have placed me incorrectly?

2420. Will I have to take remedial classes?

2421. Will I have to pay for remedial classes?

2422. Can I be exempted from remedial courses?

2423. Will my financial aid pay for remedial classes?

2424. Will remedial courses satisfy requirements for my degree?

2425. May I retake placement tests? How often?

2426. How long are placement test scores valid?

2427. Are lockers available on campus?

2428. How do I get a locker assignment?

2429. What happens if I miss orientation?

2430. What are the advantages and disadvantages of attending orientation?

2431. Who can I ask about orientation?

2432. What can I read about orientation?

2433. Who is in charge of orientation?

2434. How can I contact the orientation office?

2435. Where is the orientation office located?

2436. When is the orientation office open? Evenings? Weekends?

2437. What else should I know about orientation at this college?

Academic Advising

Types of Courses

2438. Once I am admitted to this college can I take any course I want?

2439. What is a core course?

2440. What is a required course?

2441. What is an elective course?

2442. What is a prerequisite course?

2443. What is a co-requisite course?

2444. What is a laboratory course?

2445. What is a seminar course?

2446. What is a lecture or discussion course?

2447. What is a workshop course?

2448. What is a studio course?

2449. What is a portfolio course?

2450. What is a gatekeeper course?

2451. What is a remedial course?

2452. What is a developmental course?

2453. What is an independent study course?

2454. What is a distance-learning course?

2455. Will I have to take virtual or online courses?

2456. What is a Web-based course?

2457. What is a satellite course?

2458. What is a video course?

2459. What is an interactive television course?

2460. What is a half course?

2461. What is an off-campus course?

2462. What is a weekend course?

2463. What is a correspondence course?

2464. What is a summer course?

2465. What is a first-year or freshman experience course?

2466. Is the first-year course mandatory? Optional?

2467. Is the first-year course offered for credit? No credit?

2468. What are the advantages and disadvantages of taking a first-year course?

2469. What is a learning community course?

2470. Is a learning community course mandatory? Optional?

2471. Do learning community courses require me to take several classes with the same group of students?

2472. What are the advantages and disadvantages of studying with the same students?

2473. What is a senior year course?

2474. Is the senior year course mandatory? Optional?

2475. Is the senior year course offered for credit? No credit?

2476. What are the advantages and disadvantages of taking a senior year course?

2477. What is a study abroad course?

2478. Will study abroad programs help me gain experience in my major?

2479. Where can I find information about study abroad programs?

2480. Do I need a passport to study abroad?

2481. Do I need additional medical insurance to study abroad?

2482. Do I need vaccinations?

2483. Do I need to take a medical exam?

2484. Does a study abroad course fee include tuition?

2485. How many academic credits will I earn in a study abroad course?

2486. Is faculty permission required for registration in study abroad?

2487. Does the study abroad course fee include roundtrip travel?

2488. Can I arrange my own travel?

2489. Does the fee include housing?

2490. How many people will live in a room?

2491. Does the fee include all meals?

2492. Does the fee include ground travel?

2493. Does the fee include tours and excursions?

2494. Will I need additional spending money?

2495. Can friends and family visit me abroad?

2496. Will I be able to graduate on time if I study abroad?

2497. What else should I know about the different types of courses at this college?

Course Selection

2498. Does this college assign academic advisors?

2499. Who serves as academic advisors? Faculty? Graduate students? Interns?

2500. Will my advisor be a full time faculty member?

2501. Will my advisor be a part time faculty member?

2502. Will I have an advisor if I am undecided about an academic major?

2503. Will I have an advisor if I am a non degree-seeking student?

2504. How will I be matched with an advisor?

2505. How will I be notified of the name of my advisor?

2506. When will I be notified?

2507. Will I work with the same advisor each term?

2508. Will my advisor change? How often?

2509. What is the typical advisor caseload?

2510. Is advising done in a group or on an individual basis?

2511. When are advisors available?

2512. How often must I meet with my advisor?

2513. Do I have to make an appointment?

2514. When is the best time to make an appointment?

2515. When I arrive for my meeting will my advisor have my file?

2516. Should I pick up my file elsewhere and take it to my advisor?

2517. Must I be advised in person?

2518. Can I be advised by telephone? Online?

2519. Is there a computerized advising system?

2520. Can I print my computerized records?

2521. What is the role of an academic advisor?

2522. Which academic rules, policies and procedures should I be aware of before meeting with my advisor?

2523. Are advising sheets available by intended major or classification?

2524. Should I prepare a tentative class schedule prior to meeting my advisor?

2525. Where can I locate course descriptions?

2526. Will my advisor tell me which courses I should take my first term?

2527. Will my advisor help identify my core course requirements?

2528. Will my advisor help identify the required electives for my major?

2529. Will my advisor help identify pre-requisite courses for my major?

2530. Will my advisor explain why I must take courses in a certain sequence?

2531. Will my advisor tell me when I can take courses in my major?

2532. Will my advisor help develop a term by term academic plan?

2533. Will my advisor help me select the specific courses I need for graduation?

2534. Will my advisor help me select other courses of personal interest?

2535. Will my advisor tell me which courses will not count toward graduation?

2536. Will my advisor be able to tell me about the faculty who teach my courses?

2537. Will my advisor be aware of the time required to complete the combination of classes I take in a term?

2538. Will my advisor make sure I am not taking courses I am not ready for?

2539. Can I take courses offered by another academic department in this college?

2540. Will my advisor help me make schedule adjustments?

2541. Is my advisor authorized to approve course substitutions?

2542. Is my advisor authorized to waive course requirements?

2543. Is my advisor authorized to accept course credits completed at other colleges?

2544. Will my advisor notify me of administrative or legislative changes in my academic program?

2545. Will my advisor help me set grade performance goals?

2546. Will my advisor indicate which courses must be completed with a minimum grade?

2547. Will my advisor serve as a counselor or mentor?

2548. Will my advisor discuss my interests and abilities with me?

2549. Will my advisor help me set long-term educational goals?

2550. Will my advisor help me see the relevance of my courses to my every day life and my career plans?

2551. Will my advisor recommend extra-curricular activities that are related to my educational and career goals?

2552. Will my advisor talk to me about exams, certification or licensing required to work in my declared major after graduation?

2553. Will my advisor receive my mid-term grade reports?

2554. Will my advisor monitor my academic progress?

2555. How will my advisor know if I am not doing well in my classes?

2556. Will my advisor help me make decisions about dropping a class before the deadline?

2557. Does this college have an early-warning system?

2558. Will my advisor contact me to discuss my academic progress?

2559. Will my advisor contact me if I don't register next term?

2560. Will my advisor make referrals to student and academic support services?

2561. Is seeing an academic advisor required or optional?

2562. What are the consequences of self-advising?

2563. Will my academic progress be delayed if I don't see an advisor?

2564. Will a hold be placed on my registration if I don't see an advisor?

2565. What records do advisors keep to avoid misadvising students?

2566. What recourse do I have if I am misadvised?

2567. What should I do if I don't like my academic advisor?

2568. How do I change my advisor?

2569. Are discussions with my advisor kept confidential?

2570. Is my advisor authorized to share my student records with others?

2571. What happens if my academic advisor takes a leave of absence?

2572. How are academic advisors trained?

2573. How are academic advisors evaluated?

2574. How is good advising recognized and rewarded?

2575. What are the advantages and disadvantages of getting advised?

2576. Who can I ask about advising?

2577. What can I read about advising?

2578. Who is in charge of advising?

2579. How can I contact the advising office?

2580. Where is the advising office located?

2581. When is the advising office open? Evenings? Weekends?

2582. What else should I know about academic advising at this college?

Declaring a Major

2583. What should I know about declaring a major?

2584. If I am admitted to this college will I automatically be admitted into my major program of study?

2585. What requirements are needed to declare a major?

2586. How many credits must be earned before I can declare a major?

2587. Who can help me if I don't know what I want to major in?

2588. Will my advisor help me select a major?

2589. Will my advisor periodically check to make sure I want to continue in my major?

2590. How many different majors are offered in the field of agriculture?

2591. How many different majors are offered in the field of architecture?

2592. How many different majors are offered in the field of arts and letters?

2593. How many different majors are offered in the field of biological sciences?

2594. How many different majors are offered in the field of business?

2595. How many different majors are offered in the field of communications?

2596. How many different majors are offered in the field of computer science?

2597. How many different majors are offered in the field of dentistry?

2598. How many different majors are offered in the field of economics?

2599. How many different majors are offered in the field of education?

2600. How many different majors are offered in the field of engineering?

2601. How many different majors are offered in the field of fine and applied arts?

2602. How many different majors are offered in the field of foreign service?

2603. How many different majors are offered in the field of forestry?

2604. How many different majors are offered in the health professions field?

2605. How many different majors are offered in the humanities field?

2606. How many different majors are offered in the field of journalism?

2607. How many different majors are offered in the field of kinesiology?

2608. How many different majors are offered in the field of law?

2609. How many different majors are offered in the field of library science?

2610. How many different majors are offered in the field of medicine?

2611. How many different majors are offered in the field of military science?

2612. How many different majors are offered in the field of music?

2613. How many different majors are offered in the field of nursing?

2614. How many different majors are offered in the field of pharmacy?

2615. How many different majors are offered in the field of physical or natural sciences?

2616. How many different majors are offered in the field of public affairs?

2617. How many different majors are offered in the field of philosophy?

2618. How many different majors are offered in the social sciences field?

2619. How many different majors are offered in the field of social work?

2620. How many different majors are offered in technical or occupational fields?

2621. How many different majors are offered in the field of theology or religion?

2622. How many different majors are offered in the field of veterinary medicine?

2623. How will I know I have chosen the right major?

2624. Should I choose a major to prepare me for a career?

2625. Should I choose a major because I really like the area of study?

2626. Should I choose a major because it will lead to a prestigious job?

2627. Should I choose a major because it will lead to a high paying job?

2628. Where can I find information about current salaries offered to graduates in my major?

2629. When is the deadline to declare a major?

2630. Can I select more than one major?

2631. What should I know about double majors?

2632. Can I have a major and a minor?

2633. What should I know about minors?

2634. How often do students at this college change majors?

2635. What if I change my mind about my major?

2636. What are the pros and cons of changing my major?

2637. How many times do students change their major before graduation?

2638. How do I change my major?

2639. Will I need to take additional courses if I change majors?

2640. Does this college provide assessment testing to help students decide an academic major?

2641. What should I do if my assessments show that I am better suited for another major?

2642. Who can I ask about declaring a major?

2643. What can I read about declaring a major?

2644. What else should I know about declaring a major?

Registration

2645. Are the courses I need to graduate offered each term?

2646. Are the courses I need to graduate offered each academic year?

2647. Do all departments follow the same academic calendar?

2648. Do I have to be a degree-seeking student to register for courses?

2649. How many credits are assigned to each hour I am in class?

2650. How many credits is a full-time

course load?

2651. How many credits is a part-time course load?

2652. What are the maximum and minimum number of credits I can take per term?

2653. Can I register for courses offered on any campus?

2654. When is the first day of classes each term?

2655. When is the last day of classes each term?

2656. Do all classes at this college start and end on the same day?

2657. When will I be able to register for classes?

2658. Is there an early registration period? When?

2659. Is there a regular registration week? When?

2660. Is there a late registration period? When?

2661. How far in advance of the first day of classes can current degree-seeking students register?

2662. How far in advance of the first day of classes can new degree-seeking students register?

2663. Will I receive an appointment to register? When?

2664. How will I be notified of the date I am allowed to register?

2665. What can prevent me from registering at my appointed time?

2666. Will I have a registration hold if I owe money?

2667. Will I have a registration hold if I haven't submitted a required document?

2668. Will I have a registration hold if I don't attend orientation?

2669. Will I have a registration hold if I owe money for an overdue library book?

2670. Where will I need to go to get my hold removed?

2671. How long does it take to get a hold removed?

2672. Can I register any time after my appointed time?

2673. How do administrators decide who gets to register first?

2674. Do freshman and transfer students register at the same time?

2675. Do returning students register at the same time?

2676. Will someone automatically register me for my first term?

2677. Am I eligible to receive priority registration?

2678. Can I register at any college campus location?

2679. How do I register for classes?

2680. Which forms must be completed to register?

2681. Do I have to submit a study plan?

2682. What is my student identification number?

2683. Do I have to use my Social Security number?

2684. What should I do if I don't have a Social Security number?

2685. Will my Social Security number be protected against identity theft?

2686. Where can I get a course schedule?

2687. Is the course schedule available online?

2688. Will a printed course schedule be sent to me? When?

2689. What is the course numbering system?

2690. Which level of courses should I register for?

2691. Do first year students usually register for 1000 level courses?

2692. Do sophomores usually register for

2000 level courses?

2693. Do juniors usually register for 3000 level courses?

2694. Do seniors usually register for 4000 level courses?

2695. Do graduate students usually register for 5000 and 6000 level courses?

2696. What is my course's prefix number?

2697. What is my course's section number?

2698. What is my course's reference number?

2699. Will I have to enter alternative courses?

2700. How do I complete a course registration form?

2701. Do I have to register in person?

2702. Can I register by mail?

2703. Can I register on the telephone?

2704. Can I register online?

2705. Is the course schedule available online?

2706. Am I required to register for classes online?

2707. Do I need a personal identification number (PIN) to register?

2708. What happens if I forget my PIN?

2709. How often do classes meet? Daily? Alternating days? Weekends?

2710. How many classes are scheduled during the day?

2711. How many classes are scheduled during the evening?

2712. Are more classes offered on a particular day of the week?

2713. How much time is spent in class per week?

2714. Are classes at this college hard to register for?

2715. How quickly do classes fill up?

2716. Do I need instructor permission to register for some courses? Which ones?

2717. How do I locate an instructor before classes begin?

2718. What happens if two courses I really need meet at the same time?

2719. How many students are permitted to register for each class I need?

2720. How will I know if seats are still available in a class?

2721. What happens if a course I want to take is closed?

2722. How do administrators make decisions about adding additional course sections?

2723. How long does it take to add a new course section?

2724. Will I receive a printout of my final course schedule?

2725. May I change my course schedule after I have registered? How?

2726. How do I drop or add courses?

2727. Do I have to complete a drop/add form?

2728. Do I need permission from my academic advisor to drop or add?

2729. Does obtaining permission to add a course after the deadline waive a late payment fee?

2730. What happens if I drop or add a course after the deadline?

2731. Will I be stuck with courses I don't want if I miss the drop/add deadline?

2732. When is the drop/add period?

2733. When is the last day to add a course?

2734. When is the last day to drop a course and receive a full refund?

2735. How will I be notified if the location for one of my classes has been changed?

2736. How will I be notified if one of my classes is cancelled?

2737. How far in advance will courses for the next term be available?

2738. Who can I ask about registration?

2739. What can I read about registration?

2740. Who is in charge of registration?

2741. How can I contact the registration office?

2742. Where is the registration office located?

2743. When is the registration office open? Evenings? Weekends?

2744. What else should I know about registering for classes at this college?

Academic Records

2745. What academic records are maintained on me as a student?

2746. How long are student records kept?

2747. Do I have access to my records?

2748. How long does it take to gain access to my academic records?

2749. What is this college's privacy policy?

2750. Who else has access to my records?

2751. Must I consent to have this college share my academic records with someone else?

2752. How do I change information in my academic records?

2753. How is my enrollment status determined?

2754. How many credits must I take to be classified as full-time?

2755. How many credits must I take to be classified as part-time?

2756. How is my enrollment level determined?

2757. How many credit hours must I complete to be classified a freshman?

2758. How many credit hours must I complete to be classified a sophomore?

2759. How many credit hours must I complete to be classified a junior?

2760. How many credit hours must I complete to be classified a senior?

2761. How many credit hours must I complete to be classified a graduate student?

2762. What grading system is used at this college?

2763. Does this college use a plus-and-minus grading system?

2764. Is a minus grade a passing grade for any course?

2765. Is a minus grade a passing grade for courses in my academic major?

2766. Does this college use a non-letter grading system?

2767. Is the non-letter grading system pass or fail?

2768. Is the non-letter grading system satisfactory or unsatisfactory?

2769. Is the non-letter grading system credit or no credit?

2770. How many non-letter grade courses can I take each term?

2771. How many non-letter grade courses can I take in my major?

2772. How many non-letter grade courses can I take if I am on probation?

2773. What is the total number of non-letter grade courses I can take at this college?

2774. Does this college convert non-letter grades to letter grades?

2775. Can I switch from a letter grade to a non-letter grade before a certain date?

2776. What are the advantages and disadvantages of selecting a non-letter grade?

2777. Does this college assign an absent grade if I don't attend the course?

2778. Does this college assign an incomplete or extension grade if I need more time to complete the course?

2779. Can undergraduate students receive incomplete grades?

2780. What grade will I receive if I drop a class or withdraw late?

2781. How will I know what grades I have earned in my classes?

2782. Will my grades be mailed to me?

2783. Will my grades be available online?

2784. Which student records can I access online?

2785. What grade point average is required to make the dean's list?

2786. What are the different types of grades that instructors can assign?

2787. Why is my grade point average important?

2788. Will my grade point average determine whether I can join clubs?

2789. Will my grade point average determine whether I am eligible for scholarships and grants?

2790. Will my grade point average determine whether I can hold leadership positions?

2791. Will my grade point average determine whether I am admitted into my academic major?

2792. Will my grade point average determine whether I can interview with certain employers?

2793. Will my grade point average determine whether I graduate?

2794. Are all grades included in my grade point average calculation?

2795. How is my grade point average calculated?

2796. Will grades from other colleges be included in my grade point average?

2797. What grade point average will place me on academic warning?

2798. What grade point average will place me on academic probation?

2799. What grades are required to be removed from probation?

2800. How much time do I have to be removed from probation?

2801. What grade point average will place me on academic suspension or dismissal?

2802. Does this college dismiss first year students after the first-term?

2803. How long will I be unable to register for classes if I am suspended or dismissed?

2804. Can I appeal to or petition college administrators to be reinstated?

2805. What extenuating circumstances will be considered for reinstatement?

2806. Will the death of a relative be considered?

2807. Will a personal injury or illness be considered?

2808. Will a physical disability be considered?

2809. What supporting documentation will I need to provide when I appeal?

2810. Is someone responsible for assisting me in the appeal/petition process?

2811. Will I have to apply for reinstatement when my suspension or dismissal period has ended?

2812. Will certain conditions be imposed if I am reinstated?

2813. Will I be able to pursue the same academic major when I return?

2814. What happens if my grades drop again?

2815. What is the time frame for completing my degree?

2816. How will I know if I am making satisfactory academic progress?

2817. Are my graduation requirements based on the catalog in effect the first term I enroll?

2818. If I leave college and return later must I meet the graduation requirements published in the new catalog?

2819. When will I need a copy of my college transcript?

2820. Will I need a copy if I am transferring to another college?

2821. Will I need a copy for employment purposes?

2822. Will I need a copy for insurance purposes?

2823. Will I need a copy for licensing or certification purposes?

2824. Will I need a copy for my files?

2825. How can I get a copy of my transcript?

2826. How can I get a copy of my transcript sent to a third party?

2827. How much does it cost to request transcripts?

2828. Does it cost extra to send transcripts outside of the United States?

2829. How long does it take to receive a transcript?

2830. Can I fax my transcript request?

2831. Can my transcripts be faxed to me?

2832. Can someone else pick up my transcripts for me?

2833. Is there a limit on the number of transcripts that I can request?

2834. Will my transcript be released if I have an overdue financial obligation?

2835. What grade point average is required to graduate *cum laude*?

2836. What grade point average is required to graduate *magna cum laude*?

2837. What grade point average is required to graduate *summa cum laude*?

2838. How can I make sure my records agree with the registrar's records?

2839. Who can I ask about my records?

2840. What can I read about my records?

2841. Who is in charge of student records?

2842. How do I contact the student records office?

2843. Where is the student records office located?

2844. When is the student records office open? Evenings? Weekends?

2845. What else should I know about student records at this college?

Tuition Payments

2846. How much is my term bill?

2847. Is tuition charged by the credit hour? Semester? Quarter? Yearly?

2848. Are some students charged a reduced tuition rate? Which ones?

2849. Am I eligible for reduced tuition because I live in a certain geographical area?

2850. Am I required to pay before or after I register for classes?

2851. Where do I go to pay my term bill?

2852. Can I make a payment online?

2853. Can I pay with a credit card?

2854. Can I pay using foreign currency?

2855. Can I pay using an out-of-state check?

2856. When is the last day to pay tuition and fees?

2857. By what time on the last day do I have to pay my tuition?

2858. Is there a payment drop box at the cashier's office?

2859. Is an extended tuition payment plan available?

2860. Is there a 50/50 payment plan?

2861. Are any other special payment plans or arrangements available?

2862. How is financial aid used to pay my bill?

2863. Is my tuition waived if I work as a graduate/teaching assistant or fellow?

2864. Is my tuition waived if I am an athlete?

2865. Is my tuition waived if I have a special talent sought by this college?

2866. Is my tuition waived if I am an employee of the federal, state or local government?

2867. Is my tuition waived if I begin to work for this college full time?

2868. How do I use my veterans benefits to make a payment?

2869. What happens if a third party is paying for my tuition?

2870. Will my fee payment be deferred if I am on financial aid?

2871. Will my fee payment be deferred if I am in a college prepaid tuition program?

2872. Will my fee payment be deferred if I receive veterans benefits?

2873. What happens if my fees are not paid on time?

2874. Will my classes be dropped if I don't pay on time?

2875. If I pay eventually, will my classes be reinstated?

2876. If I fail to make a payment, will I be reported to the credit bureau?

2877. If I fail to make a payment, will I be referred to a collection agency?

2878. Will it cost me more money if I am referred to a collection agency?

2879. What happens to my payment if I withdraw from the college?

2880. What is this college's refund policy?

2881. When is the deadline to withdraw and receive a full refund?

2882. When is the deadline to withdraw and receive a 75 percent refund?

2883. When is the deadline to withdraw and receive a 50 percent refund?

2884. When will I no longer be eligible for a refund?

2885. If I am owed a refund, how quickly will it be received?

2886. Can my refund be applied to future courses?

2887. Can this college collect money and pay off debts I may owe to merchants in the community?

2888. Who can I ask about paying my term bill?

2889. What can I read about paying my term bill?

2890. Who is in charge of the cashier's office?

2891. How can I contact the cashier's office?

2892. Where is the cashier's office located?

2893. When is the cashier's office open? Evenings? Weekends?

2894. What else should I know about tuition and fee payments at this college?

Fees and Fines

2895. What fees and fines do I have to pay in addition to tuition?

2896. Are extra fees charged for certain classes?

2897. Are students required to pay an activity fee?

2898. Are students required to pay an athletic fee?

2899. Are students required to pay a parking fee?

2900. Are students required to pay a health fee?

2901. Will I be fined if I don't register in person? How much?

2902. Will I be fined if I don't pay on time? How much?

2903. Will I be fined if I don't register on time?

2904. Will I be fined each time I change my schedule?

2905. Will I be charged a makeup exam fee?

2906. Will I be charged to change my major?

2907. Are fines incurred daily? Weekly? Each term? Per occurrence?

2908. Must I pay fees for services I do not use?

2909. Do I have to pay fees and fines at the time of registration?

2910. Will I have to pay a penalty for repeating a course?

2911. What other costs will I have to cover?

2912. Who can I ask about fees and fines?

2913. What can I read about fees and fines?

2914. What else should I know about fees and fines?

Textbooks

2915. Are books and materials required for my classes?

2916. Who decides the book(s) to be used for each class?

2917. When is the deadline for faculty to order textbooks for each term?

2918. How long will it take to obtain my books?

2919. Will my books arrive in time for reading assignments to be completed?

2920. Are books required on the first day of class?

2921. Where can I buy my books?

2922. Is the bookstore on campus operated by this college?

2923. Is the bookstore on campus operated by on outside contractor?

2924. How will I know which books to buy?

2925. How will I know where my book(s) are located?

2926. What information do I need to locate my books?

2927. How do I read a shelf tag?

2928. Can different books be required for different sections of the same class?

2929. What if my book is not on the shelf?

2930. Does the bookstore occasionally run out of books at the beginning of the term?

2931. When is the best time to purchase books?

2932. When is the rush period?

2933. Can I reserve my textbooks in advance?

2934. How early can I sign up to reserve my textbooks?

2935. Will the textbooks I reserve be removed from the shelf and held for me?

2936. When is the deadline to pick up reserved textbooks?

2937. How much do my books cost?

2938. Why are my books so expensive?

2939. Can I purchase used books for less money?

2940. How will I recognize a used book?

2941. Where are used books located?

2942. What are the advantages and disadvantages of buying used books?

2943. Can I find my textbooks for less money somewhere else?

2944. How can I pay for my books?

2945. Does the bookstore accept college vouchers? Credit cards? Out-of state checks?

2946. Is the cost of books included in my term bill?

2947. Where can I receive assistance paying for my books?

2948. Can I receive a discount if I work in the bookstore during peak periods?

2949. Are the textbooks I need for my classes available in the library?

2950. Does this college have a book loan program?

2951. Does this college have a short-term loan program for purchasing books?

2952. How can I obtain my books if my financial aid has not been disbursed?

2953. What is the bookstore's exchange policy?

2954. What is the bookstore's return policy?

2955. When is the deadline to exchange or return books?

2956. When is the best time to sell books back to the bookstore?

2957. How are buyback prices determined?

2958. How do I find out the buyback value of my used book?

2959. Will I receive more money for my book if it will be used the following term?

2960. What is the deadline for selling books back?

2961. Which books should I keep?

2962. What else can I purchase in the bookstore?

2963. Who can I ask about the bookstore?

2964. What can I read about the bookstore?

2965. Who is in charge of the bookstore?

2966. How do I contact the bookstore?

2967. Where is the bookstore located?

2968. When is the bookstore open? Evenings? Weekends?

2969. What else should I know about textbooks at this college?

Personal Experiences

Physical Health

2970. What should I know about personal hygiene?

2971. What should I know about keeping my body, hair, teeth and nails clean?

2972. What should I know about my diet, nutrition and eating healthy food?

2973. What foods should I eat to perform at my best?

2974. Should I avoid foods that are high in fat, salt and sugar?

2975. What beverages should I be drinking to perform at my best? Water? Juice?

2976. How do students' eating habits change in college?

2977. What should I know about how students' weight changes in college?

2978. What should I do if I am uncomfortable with my physical appearance?

2979. What should I know about eating disorders?

2980. What should I know about food addictions?

2981. Should I know how to shop for groceries?

2982. Should I know how to use kitchen appliances safely?

2983. Should I know how to cook or prepare meals?

2984. What vitamins and minerals should I take?

2985. What should I know about taking prescription drugs?

2986. What should I know about physical fitness?

2987. When is the best time to exercise?

2988. How much should I exercise in college?

2989. Which types of exercises should I do? Aerobic? Yoga? Strength training?

2990. What should I know about the importance of breathing exercises?

2991. What should I know about getting fresh air and sunshine?

2992. What should I know about the importance of stretching?

2993. What should I know about the importance of meditation?

2994. How much sleep should I get in college?

2995. What are the symptoms of sleep deprivation?

2996. What should I do if I get sick or injured on campus?

2997. What should I know about my medical history?

2998. What are college student's experiences with beer, wine and liquor on campus?

2999. What is this college's alcohol, drug and tobacco policy?

3000. What are the consequences of violating the alcohol, drug and tobacco policy?

3001. Is there an alcohol and drug awareness program on campus?

3002. Are student-sponsored programs alcohol and drug free?

3003. Do students need administrative approval to serve alcohol on campus?

3004. Are alcoholic beverages served or sold on campus?

3005. Are students required to show proof of age when purchasing alcohol on campus?

3006. What are the consequences of falsifying an identification card?

3007. Are alcohol and drugs easily accessible at this college?

3008. Where does drinking occur on campus? Off campus?

3009. Can I get drunk if I only drink beer?

3010. What kinds of drinking games are played at this college?

3011. What should I know about alcohol poisoning?

3012. What are the consequences of binge drinking?

3013. What should I know about hangovers, nausea and vomiting?

3014. What physical and psychological effects do illegal drugs have on the body?

3015. Can cocaine induce sudden death?

3016. Can marijuana increase my heart rate?

3017. Will I have to drink alcohol or do drugs to fit in at this college?

3018. How many violations of the student

code of conduct were committed by students who were under the influence of drugs or alcohol?

3019. How will I know I have a drinking or drug problem?

3020. Do I have problem if I am missing class or falling behind in my assignments?

3021. Do I have a problem if I have blackouts or forget things I said or what I did?

3022. Do I have a problem if I injure myself or someone else?

3023. Do I have a problem if I assault someone?

3024. Do I have a problem if I have unwanted sex under the influence of alcohol or drugs?

3025. Do I have a problem if I vandalize property?

3026. Do I have a problem if I do something I regret and have to apologize for it later?

3027. If drinking has been a problem in my family, am I at a greater risk for alcohol abuse?

3028. How can I help a friend who drinks too much?

3029. What should I do if a friend attempts to drink and drive?

3030. What should I do if a friend vomits, passes out or becomes violent or dangerous while drinking?

3031. Is there a detoxification program on campus?

3032. If I seek help for a drug or alcohol problem will I be reported to law enforcement officials?

3033. How many students have been hospitalized for abusing over-the-counter drugs? Which drugs?

3034. How many students have been hospitalized for using illegal drugs? Which drugs?

3035. How many students at this college have died or been killed as a result of alcohol or drug abuse?

3036. What are college students' experiences with cigarettes, cigars and chewing tobacco on campus?

3037. Is smoking permitted on campus? In classrooms? Offices?

3038. What should I know about chemical additives in cigarettes?

3039. What should I know about lung cancer?

3040. Is there a smoking cessation program on campus?

3041. How can alcohol, drugs and tobacco affect my academic performance?

3042. What health services are available on campus?

3043. What are the most common health problems students encounter?

3044. What medical support is available to me on campus?

3045. Can I be referred to a medical facility or hospital off campus?

3046. Which medical tests are performed on campus?

3047. Which physical exams can be taken on campus?

3048. Is vision screening available on campus?

3049. Is blood pressure screening available on campus?

3050. Can I receive allergy injections on campus?

3051. Can I have dental work done on campus?

3052. Can I get a mammogram on campus?

3053. Can I get a prostate exam on campus?

3054. Are over-the-counter medications available on campus?

3055. Can I have a prescription filled on campus?

3056. Should I notify the health or counseling center if I am taking medication for a psychiatric or psychological problem?

3057. What are the qualifications of the campus medical staff? Doctors? Nurses? Practitioners?

3058. What is the racial, ethnic and second language composition of the medical staff?

3059. Is the doctor an employee of the college, or on-call contractually?

3060. Is an appointment required to see a doctor?

3061. Can I walk in the health center and receive help right away?

3062. Is a visit with the doctor free?

3063. Am I required to have health insurance?

3064. Will I be required to purchase this college's insurance plan?

3065. What should my health insurance policy cover?

3066. Does the health or medical center accept my insurance policy?

3067. Will my parents be notified if I seek or need medical attention?

3068. Who should be notified if I cannot attend classes because I am sick or injured?

3069. Who can I ask about my physical health?

3070. What can I read about my physical health?

3071. Who is in charge of the health center?

3072. How can I contact the health center?

3073. When is the health center open?

3074. What if I am sick after hours or on weekends?

3075. Where is the health center located?

3076. How can my physical health affect my academic performance?

Emotional Health

3077. What experiences do students have with feeling glad, mad, sad, bad or afraid in college?

3078. What should I know about maintaining a positive attitude?

3079. What should I know about being optimistic about life?

3080. What should I know about maintaining a good sense of humor in college?

3081. What should I do if I feel everyone else is smarter than me?

3082. What should I do if I worry about submitting my assignments on time?

3083. What should I do if I am afraid to ask questions in class?

3084. What should I do if I am afraid to meet with my professor?

3085. What should I do if I begin to doubt my ability to succeed in college?

3086. What should I do if I feel I am a failure if I don't receive all "A's" in college?

3087. Who can help me cope with receiving failing grades?

3088. What should I do if I often feel lonely, isolated or rejected?

3089. What should I do if I often feel jealous or resentful?

3090. What should I do if I feel angry or frustrated with the college bureaucracy?

3091. What should I do if I feel homesick?

3092. What should I do if I feel confused or overwhelmed?

3093. What should I do if I find myself crying frequently or suddenly?

3094. What should I do if I feel my classes are boring and I have lost interest?

3095. What should I do if I feel my classes are not preparing me for the future?

3096. Who should I talk to if I feel like dropping out and getting a job?

3097. Who should I talk to if I am worried about my ability to finance my education?

3098. Who should I talk to about the death of a relative or close friend?

3099. Who should I talk to if I feel uncertain about my life after college?

3100. What can I read about my emotional health?

3101. How can my emotional health affect my academic performance?

Mental Health

3102. What experiences do students have with being able to respond appropriately to situations that arise in college?

3103. What should I know about how to solve problems?

3104. What should I know about how to make decisions?

3105. What should I know about coping with change and criticism?

3106. What should I know about worry and anxiety in college?

3107. What are the symptoms of anxiety?

3108. What are the symptoms of test anxiety?

3109. What are the symptoms of math anxiety?

3110. What are the symptoms of writing anxiety?

3111. What are the symptoms of speaking anxiety?

3112. What should I know about stress and feeling pressured in college?

3113. What should I know about the importance of self-talk?

3114. What should I know about the importance of self-esteem?

3115. What should I know about depression?

3116. What are the symptoms of depression?

3117. Who should I talk to if I feel suicidal?

3118. Who should I talk to, outside my circle of friends, if I have a problem?

3119. Is peer health counseling available on campus?

3120. Is mental health counseling available on campus?

3121. For what kinds of issues do students typically seek help?

3122. Is individual counseling available?

3123. Is group counseling available?

3124. Is it possible to speak with someone right away?

3125. Do I need to schedule an appointment?

3126. Is there a waiting list for appointments?

3127. What can I expect to happen at my first appointment?

3128. Will everything I say to counselors be kept confidential?

3129. What are the qualifications of the counseling staff?

3130. What is the racial, ethnic and second language composition of the counseling staff?

3131. What is the average counselor caseload?

3132. Does the counseling center provide psychological testing?

3133. What psychiatric support is available on campus?

3134. What psychiatric evaluations are available on campus?

3135. Who should I notify if I have a previous psychiatric history?

3136. Is crisis intervention available on campus?

3137. Will my medical records be kept confidential?

3138. Under what circumstances will my records be released without my consent?

3139. Who can I ask about mental health counseling?

3140. What can I read about mental health?

3141. Who is in charge of mental health counseling?

3142. How can I contact the mental health counseling office office?

3143. Where is the mental health counseling office located?

3144. When is the mental health counseling office open? Evenings? Weekends?

3145. How can my mental health affect my academic performance?

Interpersonal Experiences

Making Friends

3146. What experiences do students have making new friends in college?

3147. What opportunities will I have to make new friends on campus?

3148. What should I know about how to introduce myself to others?

3149. What should I know about overcoming shyness?

3150. What should I know about trying too hard to make friends?

3151. Where can I get a schedule of campus activities and social events?

3152. Where can I get a schedule of art, music, and drama events?

3153. Where can I get a schedule of lectures and panel discussions?

3154. How do I get tickets to entertainment or sports events?

3155. What experiences do students have maintaining friendships in college?

3156. What experiences do students have ending friendships in college?

3157. Will making new friends jeopardize

existing relationships I have with my high school friends?

3158. How do I handle any guilt I feel about leaving behind any friends who choose not to go to college?

3159. What should I know about grieving for the death of a friend?

3160. Who can I ask about making friends?

3161. What can I read about making friends?

3162. What else should I know about friendships at this college?

3163. How can friendships affect my academic performance?

Intimate Relationships

3164. What experiences do college students have starting intimate relationships?

3165. What experiences do college students have staying in intimate relationships?

3166. What should I know about spending all my free time with my partner?

3167. What experiences do students have ending intimate relationships?

3168. What should I know about becoming sexually active in college?

3169. What experiences do students have introducing sex into a relationship?

3170. What should I do if I feel I am not ready to have sex?

3171. What experiences do students have abstaining from sexual activity?

3172. What should I know about my partner before I have sex?

3173. What should I know about having sex with several partners just for fun?

3174. How are students who have several sex partners perceived on campus?

3175. Will my partner let others know I have sex just for fun?

3176. What should I know about having sex to make my relationship better?

3177. What should I know about having sex to prove I really love my partner?

3178. What should I know about having sex because I am afraid of losing my partner?

3179. What should I know about abstaining from sex until I am married?

3180. What should I know about different forms of contraception?

3181. What are the advantages and disadvantages of different forms of contraceptives?

3182. Can I get a prescription for birth control pills on campus?

3183. Can I get birth control pills at the health center?

3184. Is the morning-after pill available at the health center?

3185. Are intrauterine devices available at the health center?

3186. Are diaphragms available at the health center?

3187. Are spermicides available at the health center?

3188. Are condoms available at the health center?

3189. What other precautions should I take if I am sexually active?

3190. What should I do if I feel used after having sex?

3191. What should I know about homosexuality?

3192. Who can I talk to if I am uncertain about my sexual identity?

3193. What experiences do gay, lesbian, bisexual or transgender students have on campus?

3194. What should I know about sexually transmitted diseases?

3195. What should I do if I have genital irritations, pain, sores or discharge?

3196. Does this college test for sexually transmitted diseases?

3197. How many students at this college are being treated for sexually transmitted diseases? Which diseases?

3198. Are students being treated for chlamydia?

3199. Are students being treated for gonorrhea?

3200. Are students being treated for syphilis?

3201. Are students being treated for herpes?

3202. Is HIV/AIDS screening available on campus?

3203. What should I do if my partner or I become pregnant?

3204. Will I have to drop out of college if my partner or I become pregnant?

3205. What should I do if I feel pressured or threatened to have unwanted sex?

3206. What should I know about date rape or acquaintance rape?

3207. What should I know about rape drugs?

3208. How can I reduce my chances of being a sexual assault victim?

3209. Can I reduce my chances of being date raped if I am clear on verbal and non-verbal signals to my date?

3210. Can I reduce my chances of being raped if I avoid being alone with someone who is drunk, intoxicated or high?

3211. Can I reduce my chances of being raped if I avoid dark secluded areas?

3212. What should I do if I am sexually assaulted on campus?

3213. Who should I tell first?

3214. Should I report the sexual assault to the campus police?

3215. What happens after I report the assault to the police?

3216. What kind of medical attention do sexual assault victims receive?

3217. What kind of emotional support is provided to sexual assault victims?

3218. Will a college official help me through the process if I report it to the police?

3219. Is relationship counseling available on campus?

3220. Who can help me if I am having problems in an intimate relationship?

3221. Who can help me if I'm having problems in a long-distance relationship?

3222. Who can help me overcome jealousy in a relationship?

3223. Who can help me if I am experiencing infidelity or cheating in a relationship?

3224. What can I do if I am being physically abused in a relationship?

3225. Who can I talk to if I am having difficulty ending a relationship?

3226. What can I do if I am being stalked on campus?

3227. What is this college's sexual

harassment policy?

3228. What are the consequences of violating the sexual harassment policy?

3229. Who can I ask about intimate relationships?

3230. What can I read about intimate relationships?

3231. What else should I know about intimate relationships at this college?

3232. How can intimate relationships affect my academic performance?

Family Relationships

3233. What experiences do college students have leaving home?

3234. How can I prepare to say goodbye to my family?

3235. What experiences do college students have with separation anxiety?

3236. What are the symptoms of separation anxiety?

3237. What will my parents experience when I leave home?

3238. What will my siblings experience when I leave home?

3239. What are my family's expectations of me while I am in college?

3240. How often should I reasonably be in touch with my family?

3241. How often should I call, e-mail, write or visit home?

3242. How often should my family be in contact with me?

3243. Should my family visit me in college?

3244. What should I do to prepare for my family's visit?

3245. How will my relationship with my parents change when I am in college?

3246. What should I do if my parents are trying to control my life?

3247. What should I do if my parents are trying to make decisions about my academic major?

3248. What should I do if my parents are treating me like I am a young child?

3249. What should I do if my family feels I will outgrow them intellectually?

3250. What should I do if my parents think college is just like high school?

3251. What should I do if I find it hard to talk to my family about what I am experiences in college?

3252. How can I tell my family I want to change my major?

3253. How can I tell my family that I received failing grades?

3254. What are the terms of financial help provided by my family?

3255. Who can I talk to if I feel I am wasting my family's money?

3256. What experiences do students have returning home?

3257. Will I be going back to the same home that I left?

3258. What if my room at home has been rearranged or redecorated?

3259. How different is returning home during the holidays?

3260. Should I bring a friend home to meet my family?

3261. What should I do if my family dislikes any changes I have made in my appearance?

3262. What should I do if my family doesn't view me as an adult?

3263. What should I do if my parents tell me when I can go out and what time I come home?

3264. What experiences do students have living with other relatives?

3265. What experiences do college students have living with a spouse or partner?

3266. What experiences do college students have living with children?

3267. How can I involve my spouse and children in college life?

3268. What should I know about my relationship if my spouse is not college-educated?

3269. Whom should I notify if I have a family emergency?

3270. What should I know about handling a crisis at home?

3271. What should I consider when deciding whether to return home during a crisis?

3272. What is this college's policy on contacting my parents?

3273. Who can I ask about family relationships?

3274. What can I read about family relationships?

3275. What else should I know about family relationships at this college?

3276. How can family relationships affect my academic performance?

Roommates

3277. What experiences do students have living with other students?

3278. What are some of the first things my roommate and I should discuss after getting to know each other?

3279. What should I know about spending all my free time with my roommate?

3280. What kinds of conflicts do roommates encounter?

3281. What should I do if my roommate is messy and I am neat?

3282. How should roommates divide up chores?

3283. What experiences do roommates have buying food together?

3284. What experiences do roommates have sharing food they purchased independently?

3285. What should I do if my roommate is an early riser and I am a night person?

3286. What should I do if my roommate likes to sleep with the light on and I don't?

3287. What if my roommate and I disagree about how to decorate the room?

3288. What should I do if my roommate makes noise while I am sleeping?

3289. What should I do if my roommate makes noise when I am studying?

3290. What should I do if my roommate listens to music that I dislike?

3291. What should I do if my roommate is a smoker and I am not?

3292. What should I do if my roommate borrows my clothing, jewelry, money or other possessions without asking?

3293. What should I do if my roommate and I cannot agree on the room temperature?

3294. What should I do if my roommate forgets to give me my telephone messages?

3295. What should I do if my roommate invades my privacy and space?

3296. Can I build a partition to divide the room?

3297. What should I do if my roommate opens my mail or packages?

3298. What should I do if my roommate goes through my desk or dresser drawers?

3299. What should I do if my roommate steals my money?

3300. What should I do if my roommate likes to entertain others and I don't?

3301. What should I do if I don't like my roommate's friends?

3302. What should I do if I am burdened by my roommate's problems?

3303. What should I do if my roommate becomes intimate with someone else in my presence?

3304. What should I do if my roommate has overnight guests without my consent?

3305. What should I do if my roommate threatens to fight or physically harm me?

3306. What experiences do roommates have resolving their conflicts?

3307. Should roommates talk directly to each other about their concerns?

3308. Should roommates try to compromise?

3309. Should roommates put their agreements in writing?

3310. What experiences do students have living with more than one roommate?

3311. What experiences do students have living with friends who do not attend college?

3312. Who can help me if I can't resolve my roommate problems?

3313. How long should I live with an incompatible roommate before requesting a room change?

3314. What should I do if housing is filled and a room change is not possible?

3315. Who can I ask about roommates?

3316. What can I read about roommates?

3317. Who is in charge of residential housing?

3318. How can I contact current housing students?

3319. How can I contact the residential housing office?

3320. Where is the residential housing office located?

3321. When is the residential housing office open? Evenings? Weekends?

3322. What else should I know about roommates at this college?

3323. How can experiences with my roommate affect my academic performance?

Classmates

3324. What experiences do college students have with their classmates?

3325. How will my classmates differ from me?

3326. What should I know about interacting with classmates whose opinions are different from mine?

3327. What should I do if I am asked to discuss a controversial issue in class?

3328. Should I be prepared to change my opinion as a result of new information or persuasive arguments made by my classmates?

3329. How can I find out what happened in a class that I missed?

3330. Should I learn the names of some classmates in each class?

3331. Should I exchange telephone numbers with some classmates in each class?

3332. What should I know about studying in groups?

3333. Should I form or join a study group for each class?

3334. Will getting other points of view help me learn more?

3335. How many people should be in a study group?

3336. How often should a study group meet?

3337. How should a study group spend its time together?

3338. Should study group members compare their class notes?

3339. Should study group members compare their text notes?

3340. Should study group members discuss assignments?

3341. What experiences do students have working together on a group project?

3342. Does the syllabus describe group project requirements?

3343. Should the group divide large assignments into smaller ones?

3344. Will everyone in the group receive the same grade?

3345. What should I do if a group member does not complete his or her work?

3346. How strong is competition among students in the classroom?

3347. Is competition so strong that students are tempted to cheat?

3348. Will students sometimes have to critique each other's work?

3349. What should I do if a classmate monopolizes the discussion?

3350. What should I do if a classmate asks questions that have already been answered?

3351. What should I do if I am aware that other students are cheating?

3352. Does this college have an honor code?

3353. Where can I get a copy of the honor code?

3354. Is it a code violation if I submit a paper that someone else wrote for me?

3355. Is it a code violation if I buy a paper on the Internet or from someone else and submit it as my own?

3356. Is it a code violation to copy a section of a book and submit it in my paper as my own work?

3357. Is it a code violation to use the same term paper to meet the requirements for two different classes?

3358. Is it a code violation to have someone take a test for me?

3359. Who can I ask about classmates?

3360. What can I read about classmates?

3361. What else should I know about my classmates at this college?

3362. How can my experiences with classmates affect my academic performance?

FACULTY

3363. What experiences do students have with faculty members?

3364. Do students at this college choose their instructors?

3365. How do I choose an instructor?

3366. How can I contact my instructor prior to class?

3367. How do I address my instructor? First name? Doctor? Professor?

3368. What is my instructor's academic rank?

3369. Is my instructor a lecturer?

3370. Is my instructor an adjunct professor?

3371. Is my instructor an assistant professor?

3372. Is my instructor an associate professor?

3373. Is my instructor a professor?

3374. Does my professor have tenure?

3375. How long does it take a professor to receive tenure?

3376. Has my instructor written any books?

3377. Has my instructor written the book that is being used in my class?

3378. Is my instructor conducting scholarly research locally? Nationally? Overseas?

3379. Will I be able to work with my instructor on research projects?

3380. Will I have an opportunity to publish research results with my professor?

3381. Has my instructor won any awards, prizes or grants?

3382. Where did my instructor go to college?

3383. Will my instructor be approachable?

3384. Will my instructor be available to assist me outside of class?

3385. How many office hours must faculty keep per week?

3386. How will I know when my instructor holds office hours?

3387. Will office hours be posted on the instructor's door?

3388. What if my instructor does not have an office on campus?

3389. Do I need an appointment to meet with my instructor?

3390. What if my schedule conflicts with my instructor's office hours?

3391. Must I meet with a teaching assistant before seeing my instructor?

3392. Should I estimate the amount of time I will need to meet with my instructor?

3393. Should I develop a list of questions or topics before the meeting?

3394. Should I ask for study tips about the course material?

3395. Should I expect material from a missed class to be re-taught during office hours?

3396. Should I expect my instructor to photocopy or provide notes from a missed class?

3397. How will I know if my instructor is really concerned about me as a student?

3398. Will my instructor have my contact information prior to class?

3399. Will my instructor know anything about my background prior to class?

3400. Do instructors provide their home phone numbers or email addresses to students?

3401. Do faculty members serve as mentors to students?

3402. Do faculty members serve as advisors to student clubs and organizations?

3403. What is my instructor's teaching style?

3404. How can I make a good impression on my instructor?

3405. How can I avoid distracting the instructor during class?

3406. What are the consequences of arriving late or leaving early from class?

3407. What are the consequences of holding a conversation during the lecture?

3408. What are the consequences of sleeping in class?

3409. What are the consequences of acting bored in class?

3410. What are the consequences of studying for another class while in class?

3411. What are the consequences of passing notes in class?

3412. What are the consequences of talking on my cell phone in class?

3413. What are the consequences of text messaging in class?

3414. What are the consequences of missing or skipping class?

3415. If I repeatedly disrupt class or distract my instructor will I be asked to leave?

3416. What other requirements can my instructor impose?

3417. Will I be required to obtain consent from the instructor before missing a class?

3418. Will I be required to resubmit assignments until they are satisfactory?

3419. What should I do if I have a recurring medical condition that prevents me from attending class?

3420. Do instructors make exceptions for illnesses and emergencies that can be verified?

3421. Will emergencies and excused absences be handled on an individual basis?

3422. What should I do if my instructor is rigid and unsympathetic?

3423. What should I do if I contact my instructor and do not receive a timely response?

3424. What should I do if I can't contact my instructor?

3425. What should I do if my instructor does not show up for class?

3426. How long should I wait if an instructor is late for class?

3427. Do my instructors keep students past the time limit?

3428. What should I do if I can't understand what my instructor is saying?

3429. What should I do if my instructor is not well prepared and organized?

3430. What should I do if my instructor does not follow the syllabus?

3431. Does my instructor have the option of changing the syllabus?

3432. Can an instructor change course requirements as the course unfolds?

3433. What should I do if I disagree with my instructor?

3434. What is the best way to politely question my instructor's authority?

3435. What opportunities are there to socialize with an instructor outside of class?

3436. Do instructors attend social events on campus?

3437. Do instructors invite students to their homes?

3438. What experiences do students have being romantically involved with a faculty member?

3439. What should I know about having a crush on my professor?

3440. What should I do if my professor is making unwanted sexual advances toward me?

3441. What is this college's policy on becoming romantically involved with a professor?

3442. What is the procedure for filing a grievance against an instructor?

3443. Is there a deadline for filing a grievance?

3444. Can I file a grievance if an instructor does not abide by the syllabus?

3445. Can I file a grievance if an instructor engages in offensive behavior?

3446. Can I file a grievance if an instructor uses offensive language?

3447. Can I file a grievance if an instructor makes racial or stereotypical jokes?

3448. Can I file a grievance if an instructor ridicules me or other students?

3449. Can I file a grievance if an instructor discriminates based on age, sex, religion, race, marital status, national origin or disability?

3450. Can I file a grievance if an instructor uses or represents my research or scholarly work as their own?

3451. Can I file a grievance if an instructor awards grades arbitrarily?

3452. Have instructors at this college been accused of grade inflation?

3453. Are instructors limited in the number of 'A's" they can give to a class?

3454. Are instructors reluctant to give failing grades?

3455. Before I file a grievance must I first attempt to resolve the issue with my instructor?

3456. How often do professors go on sabbatical leave?

3457. When are my professors scheduled to go on sabbatical leave?

3458. What else should I know about faculty at this college?

3459. How can my experiences with the faculty affect my academic performance?

Administrators

3460. What experiences do students have with administrators at this college?

3461. Do administrators serve as mentors?

3462. Do administrators serve as advisors to student clubs and organizations?

3463. Do administrators attend student-sponsored events?

3464. Do administrators appoint students to campus committees?

3465. Which administrative policies and procedures should I know about?

3466. Where can I get a copy of the student handbook?

3467. Where can I get a copy of the student directory?

3468. Where can I get a copy of the faculty/staff directory?

3469. Where can I get an official academic calendar?

3470. Where can I get a copy of the parent handbook?

3471. Where can I get a copy of the faculty handbook?

3472. Where can I get a copy of the student code of conduct?

3473. Who implements or enforces the student code of conduct?

3474. How is the student code of conduct enforced?

3475. Does the code of conduct make me responsible for my behavior?

3476. Does the code of conduct hold me accountable for the behavior of my guests when they are on campus?

3477. Does the code of conduct apply to my behavior when I am off campus?

3478. What should I do if I am accused of misconduct?

3479. Which violations of the code can I be charged with?

3480. Is disobeying or defying a college official a violation?

3481. Is providing false information to a college official a violation?

3482. Is using profane or vulgar language or gestures a violation?

3483. Is misrepresenting myself as a college official a violation?

3484. Is falsification of records a code violation?

3485. Is pulling a fire alarm or manipulating a smoke detector a violation?

3486. Is initiating a bomb scare a violation?

3487. Is possession of firearms, explosives, combustible fuels, firecrackers or dangerous weapons a violation?

3488. Is possession of stolen goods a violation?

3489. Is being disruptive, disorderly or

creating a public disturbance a violation?

3490. Is being lewd, indecent or obscene a violation?

3491. Is smoking in an unauthorized area a violation?

3492. Is manufacturing, possessing, using or distributing illegal drugs or alcohol a violation?

3493. Is getting ticketed or arrested for drunk driving a violation?

3494. Is illegal gambling a violation?

3495. Is misuse of computers or computer networks a violation?

3496. Is bringing radioactive materials on campus a violation?

3497. Is making obscene or harassing telephone calls a violation?

3498. Is abusive behavior a code of conduct violation?

3499. Is theft and burglary a code violation?

3500. Is vandalism a code violation?

3501. Is hazing a code violation?

3502. Is assault and battery a code violation?

3503. Which violations of the academic code of conduct can I be charged with?

3504. Is cheating academic misconduct?

3505. Is plagiarism academic misconduct?

3506. Is bribery to gain academic advantage misconduct?

3507. Is unauthorized appropriation of another's computer programs misconduct?

3508. Will any charges against me be limited to campus violations?

3509. Will any charges be reported to local law enforcement authorities?

3510. Who decides the outcome of my case?

3511. Is there a judicial committee?

3512. Who are the members of the committee?

3513. How is the judicial committee appointed?

3514. How long does the committee serve? On term? An academic year?

3515. Are students members of the judicial committee?

3516. How is the judicial committee trained?

3517. How long do judicial committee members serve?

3518. Are legal services provided on campus?

3519. Can an attorney represent me at a judicial hearing?

3520. What are the investigation procedures?

3521. Will I be given due process?

3522. Is mediation an alternative to a judicial proceeding?

3523. Is conflict resolution an alternative to a judicial proceeding?

3524. Will there be a mock trial?

3525. Which type of hearing will be held? Formal? Informal?

3526. What are the hearing procedures?

3527. When are hearings scheduled?

3528. How will I be notified that a hearing has been scheduled?

3529. How long does it take to process a case?

3530. Can I be suspended until a final decision is reached?

3531. What sanctions can be imposed upon me?

3532. Is counseling a sanction?

3533. Is a reprimand a sanction?

3534. Is suspension a sanction?

3535. Is expulsion a sanction?

3536. Is restitution a sanction?

3537. Is getting arrested a possibility?

3538. Is serving time in jail a possibility?

3539. What are the appeals procedures?

3540. Will my parents be notified of my misconduct?

3541. Will my misconduct be reported to the media?

3542. Where can I get help to change my behavior?

3543. Who can I ask about administrators?

3544. What can I read about administrators?

3545. How do I contact administrators?

3546. Who is in charge of administrators?

3547. When are administrators' offices open? Evenings? Weekends?

3548. What else should I know about administrators at this college?

3549. How can relationships with administrators affect my academic performance?

Career Experiences

3550. What experiences do students have planning for careers while in college?

3551. How do I begin to make career plans?

3552. How will I know I have chosen the right major?

3553. Are career interest inventories available on campus?

3554. Are career-related personality tests available on campus?

3555. Is there a computerized career assessment program on campus?

3556. Who can help me develop a career plan?

3557. How often do students change their career plans?

3558. What career counseling services are offered on campus?

3559. Are resume-building workshops offered?

3560. Who can help me identify my career-related accomplishments?

3561. Is resume critiquing offered?

3562. Are mock interviews offered?

3563. Are majors fairs held?

3564. Are graduate school fairs held?

3565. Is business etiquette training provided?

3566. When am I eligible to take advantage of career counseling?

3567. Should I wait until my senior year to seek career counseling?

3568. Is there a career research library on campus?

3569. Where can I find information on labor/job market trends?

3570. Where can I find information on current workforce needs?

3571. Where can I find a list of professional organizations available to assist me?

3572. Where can I find company profiles?

3573. Where can I find subscriptions to newsletters or journals?

3574. Where can I find employment listings available?

3575. Where can I find job-related directories and reference books on campus?

3576. Where can I find information on equal opportunity employment laws?

3577. How can I gain real world experience within my chosen major?

3578. Will an internship or cooperative education course provide real world experience?

3579. Is an internship required for graduation?

3580. Can an internship be part time? Full time?

3581. Can an internship be on campus? Off campus?

3582. Can an internship be paid? Not paid?

3583. When can I enroll in an internship class?

3584. How can I find out which employers or agencies offer internships?

3585. How do I obtain an internship?

3586. Is an application required?

3587. Is an interview with the potential employer or agency required?

3588. Must I register for the internship as a class and pay tuition?

3589. Can I complete an internship in an area that is different from my major?

3590. Where can I find information on internships?

3591. Who will supervise my internship?

3592. How is my internship graded?

3593. Who must approve my internship?

3594. Should my internship be cited on my resume?

3595. Will leadership training help me gain real world experience?

3596. What opportunities are there to receive leadership training on campus?

3597. Is leadership training available through student government?

3598. Is leadership training available through residential housing?

3599. Will serving as a peer counselor help me gain real world experience?

3600. Will tutoring other students help me gain real world experience?

3601. Will serving as a peer advisor help me gain real world experience?

3602. Will serving as an orientation leader help me gain real world experience?

3603. What are the advantages and disadvantages of using career services?

3604. Who can I ask about career services?

3605. Are alumni mentors available in certain careers?

3606. What are the qualifications of the career services staff?

3607. What is the racial, ethnic, second language and gender composition of the career services staff?

3608. What are the academic credentials of the career services staff?

3609. How many years of experience does the staff in career services have?

3610. What can I read about career services?

3611. Who is in charge of career services?

3612. How can I contact the career services office?

3613. Where is the career services office located?

3614. Do I need to make an appointment?

3615. Can I just walk in to career services?

3616. When is the career services office open? Evenings? Weekends?

3617. How can career experiences affect my academic performance?

Financial Experiences

3618. What experiences with money do students have in college?

3619. What should I know about earning money?

3620. Where does my spending money come from?

3621. What should I know about budgeting my money in college?

3622. How should I budget for fixed expenses?

3623. How should I budget for variable expenses?

3624. Should I make a list of all my monthly and term expenses?

3625. Should I make a list of all my sources of income?

3626. Who can help me develop a budget?

3627. What should I know about advertising and consumer behavior?

3628. What should I know about getting the most for my money?

3629. What experiences do students have overspending their budget?

3630. What should I know about banking my money?

3631. What should I know about investing my money?

3632. What should I know about making donations or charitable contributions?

3633. What should I know about borrowing money?

3634. What should I know about asking my family for money?

3635. What should I know about using credit cards?

3636. What are the advantages and disadvantages of having my own credit cards?

3637. Will future employers request my credit report?

3638. Is a consumer credit counseling service available on campus? In the community?

3639. What should I know about managing my money?

3640. What should I know about paying my bills?

3641. Should my bills be paid on time?

3642. Should I pay the minimum amount due each month?

3643. Should I stay within my credit limit?

3644. Should I pay my credit card balance before interest accrues?

3645. Should I avoid late payments?

3646. Should I avoid over-my-credit-limit fees?

3647. Should I avoid over-my-balance-limit fees?

3648. Are banking services provided on campus?

3649. Am I required to use this college's banking services?

3650. Where can I get a check cashed on campus?

3651. How do I balance my checkbook?

3652. Is there an ATM machine on campus? Where?

3653. Where can I get help if I run out of money?

3654. Where can I get help if my money is stolen?

3655. Does this college have an emergency loan fund?

3656. Does this college offer a short-term loan program?

3657. What experiences do students have with gambling?

3658. How many students at this college have gambling problems?

3659. How much debt have students incurred when they leave this college?

3660. Will my debt and loan obligations exceed my expected salary?

3661. Will my debt burden make it difficult to take low-paying jobs?

3662. Will my debt burden delay my buying a home or starting a family?

3663. Who can I ask about managing my personal finances?

3664. What can I read about managing my personal finances?

3665. What else do I need to know about my finances?

3666. How can financial problems affect my academic performance?

Environmental Experiences

Campus Climate

3667. Do students feel welcome on campus?

3668. Do students enjoy being on campus?

3669. Are faculty, staff and administrators helpful?

3670. Is the bookstore staff helpful?

3671. Is the library staff helpful?

3672. Is the health services staff competent?

3673. Is the computer center staff competent?

3674. Do employees show concern for students as individuals?

3675. Do students feel they are getting what they paid for?

3676. Do employees have the funds, materials and supplies needed to help students?

3677. Do employees have the information needed to help students?

3678. Do faculty, staff and administrators keep students informed?

3679. Are employees authorized to make decisions on the spot?

3680. Are employees too busy to help students?

3681. Do students get the runaround when seeking help?

3682. Is there geographic diversity among students at this college?

3683. Is there racial diversity at this college?

3684. Is there ethnic diversity at this college?

3685. Is there language diversity at this college?

3686. Is there religious diversity at this college?

3687. Is there age diversity at this college?

3688. Is there gender diversity at this college?

3689. Are students diverse in ability?

3690. Are students diverse in economic background?

3691. Which student groups are underrepresented on campus?

3692. Are employees sensitive to the needs of underrepresented groups?

3693. Are celebrations held recognizing the achievements, food, music, art, dance, literature and lifestyles of students from different cultures?

3694. Are campus-wide programs held to promote acceptance and tolerance of other cultures?

3695. How will I benefit from interacting with students from diverse backgrounds unlike my own?

3696. Is the curriculum inclusive of underrepresented groups?

3697. Which courses will help increase my understanding of underrepresented groups?

3698. What experiences do college students have interacting with people who are different from themselves?

3699. Is the campus climate described as hostile?

3700. Is the campus climate described as indifferent?

3701. Is the campus climate described as racist?

3702. Is the campus climate described as sexist?

3703. Is the campus climate described as homophobic?

3704. Have underrepresented groups been harassed?

3705. Have underrepresented groups had objects thrown at them?

3706. Have underrepresented groups been followed or chased?

3707. Have underrepresented groups been spat upon?

3708. Have underrepresented groups been assaulted?

3709. Have underrepresented groups been victims of hate crimes?

3710. Have underrepresented groups been victims of derogatory remarks?

3711. Have underrepresented groups been victims of verbal threats?

3712. Have victims received written offensive comments?

3713. Have victims experienced property damage?

3714. Have victims been denied services?

3715. Have victims been denied campus employment?

3716. Do victims who come forward feel pressured to remain silent?

3717. Have victims received threats of physical violence?

3718. Have victims feared for their physical safety?

3719. Where do students encounter insensitivity on campus?

3720. Have students experienced insensitivity in the residence halls?

3721. Have students experienced insensitivity in the classroom?

3722. Have students experienced insensitivity at campus events?

3723. Have students experienced insensitivity in the workplace?

3724. Is there freedom of expression on campus?

3725. Are processes in place for students to make complaints?

3726. Do students experience retaliation for expressing their opinions?

3727. What should I know about recognizing and confronting discrimination?

3728. How should I respond to others who make racial, religious or stereotypical jokes?

3729. Who can I talk to if I am uncomfortable interacting with people of different races, religions or cultures?

3730. What should I do if I experience racial or sexual harassment?

3731. What should I do if I feel uncomfortable acknowledging my cultural heritage on campus?

3732. Where can I get help adjusting to the beliefs, values and traditions of U.S. culture?

3733. How does this college address issues related to campus climate?

3734. Do students think the college responds rapidly to acts of intolerance?

3735. Do students think the college responds appropriately to acts of intolerance?

3736. Does this college provide sensitivity training?

3737. Is there a safe space or meeting place on campus?

3738. What is this college's policy on racial discrimination and hate speech?

3739. What are the consequences of violating the policy?

3740. Is there a designated advocate on campus for students who experience discrimination?

3741. Does this college survey or interview students about their perceptions of the campus climate?

3742. Who can I ask about the campus climate?

3743. What can I read about the campus climate?

3744. Who is in charge of monitoring the campus climate?

3745. What else should I know about campus climate at this college?

Campus Safety

3746. How safe am I on campus?

3747. How safe am I in the surrounding community?

3748. What experiences do students have with crime on campus?

3749. What can I do to protect myself on campus?

3750. What can I do to protect my personal property on campus?

3751. What can I do to protect my car on campus?

3752. What are the qualifications of campus police?

3753. Are campus police sworn law enforcement officers?

3754. Are campus police private security officers?

3755. Do campus police carry guns or other weapons?

3756. What partnerships exist between campus police and community police?

3757. Who responds when I call 911 on campus? Campus police? Community police?

3758. How many years of experience must campus police have?

3759. Is there an evening police escort service on campus?

3760. Do escorts work in pairs?

3761. Are escorts professionally trained?

3762. Are escorts volunteers or paid employees?

3763. Are emergency "blue light" phones available throughout the campus?

3764. Are walk paths lighted at night?

3765. How frequently is the campus patrolled?

3766. Is there a safety orientation program?

3767. What are this college's crime statistics?

3768. How many tragedies occurred on campus?

3769. How many murders were reported on campus last year?

3770. How many suicides occurred on campus?

3771. How many reports of manslaughter occurred on campus?

3772. How many forcible rapes were reported?

3773. How many statutory rapes were reported?

3774. How many robberies were reported?

3775. How many aggravated assaults were reported?

3776. How many burglaries were reported?

3777. How many motor vehicle thefts were reported?

3778. How many acts of arson were reported?

3779. How many crimes involving bodily injury were reported?

3780. How many liquor law violations were reported?

3781. How many drug law violations were reported?

3782. How many illegal weapons possessions were reported?

3783. How many rallies or protests were held on campus?

3784. What are the security policies and procedures?

3785. How strictly are campus rules enforced?

3786. Who can I ask about campus safety?

3787. What can I read about campus safety?

3788. Who is in charge of campus safety?

3789. How can I contact the campus safety office?

3790. Where is the campus safety office located?

3791. When is the campus safety office open? Evenings? Weekends?

3792. What else should I know about the campus safety environment?

3793. How can campus safety affect my academic performance?

Academic Experiences

Seeking Information

Classes

3794. What experiences do students have in the classroom?

3795. How demanding is the coursework?

3796. How is the coursework at this college different from high school?

3797. What is the first week of classes like?

3798. What should I do if I registered for a class and my name is not on the list of enrollees?

3799. Will I be automatically dropped from a class if I enrolled but never paid?

3800. Will I be automatically dropped from a class if I enrolled but never attended?

3801. Will I be automatically dropped from a class if I paid but never attended?

3802. What should I do if my class is cancelled?

3803. How will a cancelled class affect my graduation timetable?

3804. How will I know when the class will be offered again?

3805. What should I know about being in class with hundreds of other students?

3806. What experiences do students have with distance learning such as online, video, CD-ROM or two-way transmission courses?

3807. Do online courses require less work than classroom courses?

3808. Do online courses alleviate course conflict problems during registration?

3809. How will I know if an online course is right for me?

3810. Should I take an online course if I prefer direct instructor supervision?

3811. Should I take an online course if I tend to procrastinate?

3812. Should I take an online course if I prefer to have things explained verbally?

3813. Should I take an online course if I prefer to interact directly with classmates?

3814. What special skills and abilities do I need for an online class?

3815. Must I know how to use a standard computer?

3816. Must I know how to create, save and manage files on the computer?

3817. Must I know how to install software?

3818. Must I know how to access the Internet?

3819. Must I know how to use an Internet search engine?

3820. Must I have access to email and the World Wide Web?

3821. Must I know how to send and receive email messages?

3822. Must I know how to paste text from one document to another?

3823. Must I know how to download and open an attachment?

3824. Will I have to know how to submit course assignments electronically?

3825. Will I be required to participate in class-related online chats and discussions?

3826. Will I be required to know how to get my computer fixed if I experience problems?

3827. Are computer problems a legitimate excuse for late submission of online course assignments?

3828. What computer hardware and software will I need for online courses?

3829. Must I subscribe to a certain Internet provider?

3830. Can I take more than one online course at a time?

3831. Will I have to be online at a designated time?

3832. Will all students in my online course have to be online at the same time?

3833. How much time will an online course require?

3834. Where can I take an online course if I do not have a computer at home?

3835. What should I do if I have trouble accessing an online course?

3836. Will I be required to come on campus to take midterm or final exams?

3837. How will I know what my instructors expect of me?

3838. What is a syllabus?

3839. Does the syllabus describe the class rules and expectations?

3840. Will I receive a course syllabus for each class?

3841. How early can I receive my syllabus?

3842. Will I receive the syllabus early enough

to make decisions about which combination of courses I want to take in a term?

3843. Will the syllabus describe the course objectives?

3844. Will the syllabus list required and optional books I must purchase?

3845. Should I bring my books to class on the first day?

3846. Does the syllabus list any other materials required for the course?

3847. Does the syllabus describe materials placed in the reserve section of the library?

3848. Does the syllabus describe the college's class attendance and tardiness policy?

3849. Does the syllabus describe the instructor's attendance and tardiness policy?

3850. Must I go to class on the first day?

3851. Does the syllabus identify holidays?

3852. Are instructors required to accommodate religious holy days and holidays?

3853. Does the syllabus outline the reading assignments due for each class meeting?

3854. Does the syllabus outline the writing assignments due for each class meeting?

3855. Should my writing assignments be typed, bound or stapled?

3856. Does the syllabus outline the problem sets due for each class meeting?

3857. Does the syllabus outline experiments due for each class meeting?

3858. Does the syllabus outline what will be covered on the exam?

3859. Is equal importance given to information from class sessions and texts?

3860. Does the syllabus describe class participation requirements?

3861. Does the syllabus describe how much work is required outside of class?

3862. Does the syllabus describe required participation in campus and community events and activities?

3863. Must the activities I choose to attend be approved in advance?

3864. Will I have to sign a release form agreeing to accept any risks involved in an off-campus course requirement?

3865. Where should I sit in college classes?

3866. How often should I ask questions in class?

3867. Can I ask the instructor to repeat what he/she said if I did not hear or understand it?

3868. How often should I voice my opinion in class?

3869. How will I know I am doing well in class?

3870. Will the syllabus outline the grading scale?

3871. How will I be graded in each class?

3872. What is the course grading scale?

3873. Is grading based on tests alone?

3874. Is grading based on student projects?

3875. Is grading based on a point system?

3876. Is grading based on a percentage system?

3877. Is grading based on a curve?

3878. Will my grade be lowered if I submit assignments late?

3879. Will my grade be lowered if I am late to class a certain number of times?

3880. Will my grade be lowered if I miss class?

3881. Will I fail the course if I miss a certain number of classes?

3882. Which assignments are worth a higher percentage of my final grade?

3883. How often will I receive feedback on assignments and exams?

3884. Will my assignments and exams be returned at the next class period?

3885. If I am absent can I pick up my assignment or exam in my instructor's office?

3886. What happens if I miss an exam?

3887. Is there on campus an testing center that administers instructor-prepared exams?

3888. What other services are provided by the testing center?

3889. Will I have some indication of my course grades prior to the drop/add deadline?

3890. What should I do if I miss a class?

3891. What should I do if I am falling behind in class?

3892. Is there a tutoring or learning assistance center on campus?

3893. Are tutorial services limited to students who are failing?

3894. Should I seek tutoring if I am making good grades?

3895. What services are provided in the tutoring or learning center?

3896. Where is the tutoring or learning center located?

3897. When is the tutoring or learning center open? Evenings? Weekends?

3898. Do I need an appointment for tutoring?

3899. How can I contact the tutoring or learning center?

3900. Is free tutoring available? In which subjects?

3901. What are the qualifications of the tutors?

3902. What is the racial, ethnic and second language makeup of the tutoring staff?

3903. How can I make an appointment with a tutor?

3904. Will tutors help me identify my skill deficiencies?

3905. Will tutors monitor my progress throughout the term?

3906. Under what circumstances should I consider dropping a course?

3907. How can I drop a course if the drop deadline date has passed?

3908. When should I withdraw from a class?

3909. If I withdraw from one class must I withdraw from all my classes?

3910. Must I document an extreme hardship to withdraw?

3911. Can I withdraw simply because I am failing the course?

3912. When should I request an incomplete grade?

3913. What are the rules for receiving an incomplete grade?

3914. Should I complete most of the coursework to be eligible for an incomplete?

3915. Should I be passing the course to be eligible for an incomplete?

3916. How long do I have to remove an incomplete grade?

3917. How will I know my final course grade?

3918. When will my grades be posted?

3919. How will my grades be received?

3920. Will my grades be posted on the instructor's office door?

3921. Can the instructor's secretary tell me my grade?

3922. Will my grades be mailed?

3923. Can I get my grades online?

3924. Will my grades be sent to my parents?

3925. If I fail a class, can I take it again?

3926. How does repeating or retaking a class affect my grade point average?

3927. If I repeat a class, will the higher grade replace the lower grade?

3928. Is there a deadline for requesting grade forgiveness?

3929. What impact will repeating a class have on my financial aid?

3930. Will I have to pay for a repeated class out of my own pocket?

3931. Is there a limit on the number of times I can retake the same course?

3932. Is there a limit on the number of times I can retake different courses?

3933. How do I question an instructor about a grade?

3934. When must my professor submit final grades to the registrar?

3935. Can my grade be changed after my professor submits his/her grade sheet?

3936. Can I appeal a grade I don't agree with?

3937. What is the procedure for appealing a grade?

3938. When is the deadline for appealing a grade?

3939. How long do instructors keep grade books, assignments and exams?

3940. Do students at this college rate or evaluate instructors?

3941. Are course evaluations administered by the instructor? A volunteer?

3942. Will my instructor have access to course evaluations before final grades are submitted?

3943. Are faculty evaluation results available to students?

3944. How can I obtain a copy of student evaluations?

3945. Who can I ask about classes?

3946. What can I read about classes?

3947. How will attending classes affect my academic performance?

3948. What else should I know about classes at this college?

Library Services

3949. What experiences do students having using the library at this college?

3950. How much time do students in my intended major spend in the library?

3951. Where is the library?

3952. Is there more than one library on campus?

3953. Who can use the library?

3954. How many bound volumes are in the library?

3955. How many microforms are in the library?

3956. How many serials are in the library?

3957. How many commercial online services are available to students?

3958. Which audiovisual materials are available to students?

3959. What support services are provided?

3960. Which special collections are in the library?

3961. Are full-text journal articles available in the library?

3962. What materials does the library loan to students?

3963. How do I get a library card?

3964. What happens if I lose my library card?

3965. Is there a library card replacement fee?

3966. Will a lost library card be replaced immediately?

3967. Will I get a temporary card so I can continue to borrow items?

3968. Am I responsible for items checked out on my library card by someone else?

3969. Is there a limit on the number of items that can be borrowed?

3970. What happens if the information I need is not available in the library?

3971. Does the library have an interlibrary loan service?

3972. How long will it take to obtain books from other libraries?

3973. Can someone recall a book I have borrowed?

3974. Must a recalled book be returned sooner than expected?

3975. Will the library purchase items I need if they are not in the collection?

3976. How do I find items in the library?

3977. How do I obtain items that my instructor has placed on reserve?

3978. Can reserve items be taken out of the library?

3979. Are there any restrictions on reserve items?

3980. Where are the items in my intended major located?

3981. Where can I find periodicals?

3982. Where can I find audio-visual and media resources?

3983. Where can I find documents and maps?

3984. Where can I find rare books?

3985. Is a map of the library available?

3986. Is the library catalog computerized?

3987. Can I use computer and printing resources at the library?

3988. Do I need an access code for the library?

3989. How long can I keep a borrowed item?

3990. Does the length of time I can keep an item vary?

3991. How much are overdue book fines?

3992. How much are lost book fines?

3993. Where do students study in the library?

3994. What supplies should I bring to the library?

3995. Is there a designated quiet study area in the library?

3996. Are individual study carrels available?

3997. Are private group-study rooms available?

3998. Are library tours conducted?

3999. How do I schedule a library tour?

4000. Is there an online tour or tutorial?

4001. How do I access library resources from off campus?

4002. Are workshops held on research techniques? When?

4003. Are workshops held on Internet research? When?

4004. Are photocopiers available in the library?

4005. Are printers available in the library?

4006. How much does it cost to photocopy or print?

4007. Is change available at the circulation desk? Are coin changers available?

4008. Are public telephones located in the library?

4009. Are campus phones located in the library?

4010. Can I use my cell phone in the library?

4011. Are restrooms located on each floor?

4012. Are library hours extended during midterm or final exams?

4013. Who can I ask about library services?

4014. What can I read about the library?

4015. Who is in charge of the library?

4016. How can I contact the library?

4017. Where is the library office located?

4018. When is the library open? Evenings? Weekends?

4019. What else should I know about using the library at this college?

4020. How will using the library affect my academic performance?

Computer Services

4021. What experiences do students have using the computer center on campus?

4022. What services are provided in the computer center?

4023. What type of Internet access is available through the computer center?

4024. What should I know about e-mail etiquette?

4025. Am I required to have a college e-mail account?

4026. Can I also have a commercial e-mail account?

4027. How do I get a college e-mail account?

4028. Will I receive all official college announcements via e-mail?

4029. Does this college provide each student with a computer?

4030. If I already own a computer, can it be used instead?

4031. Am I required to buy or lease my own desktop or laptop computer?

4032. Am I required to buy or lease a computer from this college?

4033. What type of computer should I buy?

4034. Is dial-up access to computer resources available?

4035. Is there a wireless network on campus?

4036. How do I connect my computer to the college's network?

4037. Do I have to pay to use the college network?

4038. What type of virus protection will I have?

4039. Do I need an antivirus program on my computer?

4040. Can computers be accessed on campus? Where?

4041. How many workstations or terminals are available on campus?

4042. Is the computer lab a PC environment? Macintosh environment?

4043. Which computer applications and programs should I know?

4044. Which software programs are loaded on the campus computers?

4045. Is word processing software available in the computer lab?

4046. Is a spreadsheet program available in the computer lab?

4047. Is a graphics arts program available in the computer lab?

4048. Is a Website development program available in the computer lab?

4049. Are databases related to my intended major available in the computer lab?

4050. How can time be reserved on a computer?

4051. How many hours can I spend on a computer each day?

4052. How far in advance can I reserve a computer?

4053. If I show up late will I forfeit my reservation?

4054. Is there a help desk located in the computer lab?

4055. Are there any restrictions in the computer lab?

4056. Will I have Internet access in the computer lab?

4057. Can I type and print my papers in the computer lab?

4058. Does the computer center sell computers at a discounted price?

4059. Does the computer center repair computers?

4060. Does the computer center sell software at a discounted price?

4061. Does the computer center sell computer supplies at discount prices?

4062. What is this college's computer use policy?

4063. What are the consequences of violating the computer use policy?

4064. Who can I ask about the computer lab?

4065. What can I read about the computer lab?

4066. How can I contact the computer lab?

4067. Where is the computer lab located?

4068. When is the computer lab open? Evenings? Weekends?

4069. What else should I know about the computer center at this college?

4070. How will my ability to seek information affect my academic performance?

Recording Information

4071. What experiences do students have taking notes in class?

4072. Does this college recommend use of a particular note-taking method?

4073. Should I use an outline method?

4074. Should I use concept maps?

4075. Should I keep my notes in a loose-leaf binder? What size?

4076. Should I have a separate binder for each course?

4077. Should I write with a pencil? Ballpoint pen? Felt-tip pen?

4078. Should I write on only one side of my paper?

4079. Am I permitted to audiotape class lectures?

4080. What are the advantages and disadvantages of tape-recording classes?

4081. Should I take class notes directly on a computer?

4082. What are the advantages and disadvantages of taking notes on a computer?

4083. Should I sit front and center?

4084. Should I have a good view of the instructor?

4085. What should I listen for during class?

4086. Should I make sure the class given is the same as the class indicated on the syllabus?

4087. Should I listen for the main idea during class? New ideas?

4088. Should I listen for opening class comments?

4089. Should I listen for a certain number of details during class?

4090. Should I listen for examples during class?

4091. Should I observe the instructor's body language? Gestures? Facial expressions?

4092. Should I write down everything written on the chalkboard or overheads?

4093. Should I pay attention when the instructor's voice is raised?

4094. Should I pay attention when the instructor repeats something?

4095. What common abbreviations should I know?

4096. Can I invent my own shorthand system?

4097. Should I date and number each note page?

4098. Should I try to write what the instructor says word for word?

4099. Should I try to summarize and paraphrase what the instructor says?

4100. Should I write down questions asked by classmates?

4101. If I miss something, should I leave a blank space in my notes and fill it in later?

4102. What should I know about taking notes in math and science courses?

4103. Should I take notes when completing my reading assignments?

4104. How much time should I spend reviewing my notes?

4105. How frequently should I review my notes?

4106. Should my notes be reviewed and corrected right after class?

4107. Should my notes be reviewed before studying?

4108. Should my notes be reviewed from the previous class first?

4109. Should my notes be rewritten?

4110. What should I do if my notes are not legible or I can't read my handwriting?

4111. How will I know that my notes are accurate?

4112. Should I compare or exchange notes with a classmate to fill in missing information?

4113. Should I discuss my notes with the instructor?

4114. Does this college offer notetaking workshops?

4115. What should I know about taking notes while I am reading an assignment?

4116. Should I take notes in the margins of textbooks?

4117. Who can I ask about notetaking?

4118. What can I read about notetaking?

4119. What else should I know about notetaking?

4120. How will my ability to take notes affect my academic performance?

Studying Information

4121. What experiences do students have preparing for class?

4122. How many hours per week do students study at this college?

4123. How much study time will I need for each face-to-face course?

4124. How much study time will I need for each of my online courses?

4125. How do students at this college organize their days?

4126. What should I know about managing my time?

4127. Should I monitor how I spend my time?

4128. What should I know about developing a study schedule?

4129. When is the best time to study? Days? Evenings?

4130. How much out-of-class study time should I schedule for each hour I am in class?

4131. Should I set aside specific hours each day to study?

4132. Should I set aside specific hours each week to review each class?

4133. What kind of appointment calendar should I use?

4134. What are the advantages and disadvantages of using a paper calendar?

4135. What are the advantages and disadvantages of using an electronic calendar?

4136. What are the advantages and disadvantages of using a computerized calendar?

4137. Which activities should be scheduled as fixed time? Classes? Work? Study? Sacred?

4138. Which activities should be scheduled as flexible time? Eating? Sleeping? Chores?

4139. Which activities should be scheduled as free time? Socializing? Entertainment?

4140. Should I assign more study time to subjects that require greater preparation?

4141. Should I adjust my work schedule based on my course load?

4142. How should I keep track of all my assignment due dates for the term?

4143. Who can I ask for help in developing a daily, weekly and term study schedule?

4144. Who can help me identify my biggest time-wasters?

4145. What should I know about my study environment?

4146. Should my study environment be used for study only?

4147. Where is the best place for me to study?

4148. Which reference books should I keep in my study area? A thesaurus? Style manual? Dictionary?

4149. What should I know about the lighting, temperature, and furniture in my study area?

4150. How should I prioritize my time?

4151. Should I plan to read a certain number of pages or complete a certain number of problems during a study session?

4152. Should I identify how much I want to complete by the end of each study session?

4153. Should I study my most difficult subjects first?

4154. Should my assignments be broken down into manageable parts?

4155. What study method should I use?

4156. Should I preview all class materials?

4157. Should I make a list of questions that come to mind during my preview?

4158. What should I know about reading textbooks and other written materials?

4159. How much reading is required for each class?

4160. How can I learn to read faster?

4161. Is a speed-reading course available on campus?

4162. What should I know about how to read textbooks?

4163. Should I scan the title page?

4164. Should I scan the copyright page?

4165. Should I scan the table of contents?

4166. Should I scan the preface and introduction?

4167. Should I scan the chapter summaries?

4168. Should I scan the appendix?

4169. Should I scan the glossary?

4170. Should I scan the footnotes or references?

4171. Should I scan the name index?

4172. Should I scan the subject index?

4173. How should I preview a chapter?

4174. Should I read the chapter headings and subheadings?

4175. Should I translate headings into questions?

4176. Should I preview illustrations, photos, tables and figures?

4177. Should I read chapter summaries?

4178. Should I complete practice problems?

4179. Should I pay attention to words or numerals printed in italics or boldface?

4180. How should I interpret diagrams?

4181. How should I interpret pie charts?

4182. How should I interpret bar graphs?

4183. How should I interpret line graphs?

4184. How should I interpret tables?

4185. How should I interpret timelines?

4186. How should I interpret concept maps?

4187. Should I translate what I see into my own words?

4188. What should I do if I see an unfamiliar term in my reading?

4189. What should I do if I start day-dreaming while reading a passage?

4190. What should I do if I find myself reading a passage over and over?

4191. What should I do if it takes me a long time to read and comprehend assignments?

4192. How many times should I read an assignment?

4193. Should I restate what I read in my own words?

4194. Should I recite or say what I read out loud?

4195. Should I have an internal dialogue about what I read?

4196. When should I take a break?

4197. How should I highlight or mark my textbook?

4198. Should I highlight or underline key words and main ideas?

4199. What should I know about procrastination?

4200. Should I avoid studying because I am afraid I won't do the assignment correctly?

4201. Should I avoid studying because I work well under pressure?

4202. Should I avoid studying because I don't know how to complete the assignment?

4203. Should I avoid studying because the assignment seems too hard?

4204. Should I avoid studying because I am not in to mood?

4205. Should I avoid studying because I am tired?

4206. Should I avoid studying because I want to do something else?

4207. What should I know about trying to cram everything in at the last minute?

4208. What should I know about studying for math and science classes?

4209. What should I know about memorizing math formulas?

4210. What should I know about solving

math problems?

4211. What should I know about studying scientific theories or concepts?

4212. What should I know about using scientific or laboratory equipment?

4213. What should I know about experimental procedures?

4214. What should I know about my preferred learning style?

4215. Does this college administer a learning styles assessment?

4216. How will I know if I prefer to learn by seeing?

4217. How will I know if I prefer to learn by hearing?

4218. How will I know if I prefer to learn by touching?

4219. How will I know if I prefer to learn by using my right brain?

4220. How will I know if I prefer to learn by using my left brain?

4221. How will I know if I prefer to learn by experiencing?

4222. How will I know if I prefer to learn by reflecting?

4223. How will I know if I prefer to learn by thinking?

4224. How will I know if I prefer to learn by doing?

4225. Which learning styles should I improve?

4226. What should I know about studying in a group?

4227. Does this college offer workshops in study skills?

4228. Who can I ask about studying?

4229. What can I read about studying?

4230. What else should I know about studying?

4231. How will my ability to study affect my academic performance?

Recalling Information

4232. What is the best way to remember what I learn?

4233. What strategies can I use to improve my memory?

4234. What experiences do students have concentrating on what they are studying?

4235. How long is the average person's concentration span?

4236. What if I find it difficult to concentrate while I am reading?

4237. How can I create a distraction-free study area ?

4238. How can I silence inner chatter?

4239. What will distract me internally while studying? Worry? Stress? Lack of interest?

4240. What will distract me externally while studying? Noise? Temperature? Friends? Photos? Clocks?

4241. What kind of music can stimulate learning?

4242. What kind of music can cause distraction or fatigue?

4243. How can the number of distractions I encounter be minimized?

4244. How can I create an interruption-free study area?

4245. How can I keep my mind from wandering when I study?

4246. Should I monitor the thoughts that distract me?

4247. Should I write those thoughts down with the intention of coming back to them?

4248. What experiences do students in college have remembering what they learn?

4249. How does memory work?

4250. Do students in my intended major use specific memory techniques?

4251. How is information stored in the brain?

4252. How is information retrieved from the brain?

4253. Does reviewing help me recall material?

4254. Does repetition help me recall material?

4255. Does reciting help me recall material?

4256. Does explaining the material to someone else help my recall?

4257. How can my short-term memory be improved? Rest periodically?

4258. How can my long-term memory be improved? Review weekly?

4259. Should I associate material I am learning with something I already know?

4260. Should I study information over and over?

4261. How many times should I reread information that is new?

4262. What are mnemonic devices?

4263. Should I use mnemonics?

4264. Should I create acronyms?

4265. Should I use chaining?

4266. Should I use association?

4267. Should I create acrostics?

4268. Should I prepare index cards as study aids?

4269. Should I make and use flash cards?

4270. Who can I ask about improving my memory?

4271. What can I read about improving my memory?

4272. What else should I know about memory techniques?

4273. How will my ability to remember affect my academic performance?

Transmitting Information

Taking Exams

4274. What experiences do students have taking tests, exams or quizzes?

4275. Are fewer tests given in college than in high school?

4276. What should I do before a test?

4277. How will I find out what material will be covered on a test?

4278. What should I bring to the test? A calculator, dictionary, scrap paper, formulas, notes? Open book?

4279. How will I know the types of questions that will be asked?

4280. How will I know how many questions will be asked?

4281. Should I make a list of questions that I predict will be on the test?

4282. Are copies of old exams available?

4283. What are objective tests?

4284. What should I know about how to take objective tests?

4285. What should I know about taking multiple-choice tests?

4286. Should I eliminate answers that I know are wrong?

4287. Should I notice choices such as "all" and "only"?

4288. Should I answer questions that are easiest for me first?

4289. What should I know about taking fill-in-the-blank tests?

4290. What are subjective tests?

4291. What should I know about how to take subjective tests?

4292. Should I write with a pencil on essay tests?

4293. What words should I pay attention to in the directions? Describe? Outline? Summarize? Define? Analyze?

4294. How do I answer "compare and contrast" questions?

4295. How do I answer "cause and effect" questions?

4296. How do I answer chain-of-events questions?

4297. What should I know about answering essay questions?

4298. What strategies should I use to complete math and science problems?

4299. How will I know which questions to attempt to answer?

4300. How will I know which questions to omit?

4301. What are some causes of test anxiety? Fear of failure? Low self-esteem? Inadequate preparation? Worry about not meeting parents' expectations?

4302. Do the symptoms of test anxiety include sweaty palms? Nausea? Headaches? Nervousness?

4303. How do I overcome test anxiety?

4304. Does preparing well in advance help eliminate text anxiety?

4305. Does positive self-talk help eliminate test anxiety?

4306. Do breathing and relaxation techniques help eliminate test anxiety?

4307. Does concentration and meditation help eliminate test anxiety?

4308. Does creative visualization help eliminate text anxiety?

4309. What should I do during a test?

4310. Should I survey the entire test first?

4311. Should I write down facts and formulas I memorized?

4312. How should I pace myself during an exam?

4313. Should I answer all the easy questions first?

4314. Should I guess if there is no penalty for wrong answers?

4315. Should I check my work for errors?

4316. Should I use all the time provided for the test?

4317. What should I know about taking true-false tests?

4318. What should I do after a test?

4319. Does the syllabus list dates for quizzes, midterm and final exams?

4320. Is the teaching schedule the same as the final exam schedule?

4321. Are the midterm and final exams administered by someone other than the instructor?

4322. Does the syllabus describe the format of all exams?

4323. Does the syllabus describe the material to be covered on each quiz, midterm and final exam?

4324. Does the syllabus specify the building and room number where the exam will be given?

4325. Will the final exam be given during a regularly scheduled class period?

4326. Will an exam be open-book? Take-home?

4327. Are open-book and take-home exams harder?

4328. Will I need a bluebook for an exam?

4329. Will I need scanning sheets for an exam? Which color?

4330. Does the syllabus describe the consequences of missing an exam?

4331. What happens if I need to leave the room during an exam?

4332. Does the syllabus describe the instructor's policy for makeup exams or alternative testing dates?

4333. What should I do if I have two exams scheduled on the same day?

4334. Can books, notes, handouts and or calculators be used during a test?

4335. After an exam, should I compare the test questions on the test with the study questions I developed?

4336. Should I review what was answered correctly?

4337. Should I note areas requiring improvement?

4338. Should I time myself?

4339. Who can I ask about taking exams?

4340. What can I read about taking exams?

4341. Who is in charge of the testing center?

4342. How can I contact the testing center office?

4343. Where is the testing center office located?

4344. When is the testing center office open? Evenings? Weekends?

4345. What else should I know about exams?

4346. How will my ability to take exams affect my academic performance?

Research Papers

4347. What experiences do students have writing papers?

4348. Does the syllabus provide guidelines for written assignments?

4349. Must writing assignments be typed, double-spaced, a certain number of pages and/or use specific margins, fonts, type sizes or reference citations?

4350. What should I know about writing research papers?

4351. How do I choose a research paper topic?

4352. Should I consider writing about something I already know but want to learn more?

4353. Should I write about something I know nothing about but want to investigate?

4354. Does my term paper topic need to be approved in advance?

4355. Where should I search for information for my paper?

4356. Should I search for information in books? Encyclopedias?

4357. Should I search for information on the Internet?

4358. Should I search for information in newspapers, magazines and journals?

4359. Will interviews, surveys or questionnaires provide information for my paper?

4360. How do I start putting what I find into my own words?

4361. When should I start writing papers? Immediately?

4362. How do I write a thesis statement?

4363. How should I organize or synthesize the ideas, facts and questions in my paper?

4364. Must my sources be relevant to the assigned topic?

4365. Must the information be timely and up-to-date?

4366. How do I write a conclusion based on what I find?

4367. How far in advance of the due date should a first draft be completed?

4368. How far in advance of the due date should a final draft be completed?

4369. Which reference books should I consult when writing a paper? Dictionary? Thesaurus? Book of quotations? Grammar handbook? Stylebook?

4370. Does my intended major use the *Publishing Manual of the American Psychological Association?*

4371. Does my intended major use the *MLA Style Manual and Guide to Scholarly Publishing?*

4372. Does my intended major use *The Chicago Manual of Style*?

4373. Does my intended major use *The Associated Press Stylebook and Briefing on Media Law*?

4374. How should I document my sources of information?

4375. How should I cite footnotes?

4376. How should I prepare a bibliography?

4377. How should I cite references?

4378. How can I check my spelling,

grammar, organization and paragraph structure?

4379. Should I use the computer spellcheck function?

4380. Should I use a grammar check?

4381. Should I read my final draft out loud to catch any errors?

4382. Does the syllabus define plagiarism and its consequences?

4383. What happens if I commit plagiarism when preparing my paper?

4384. Who can I ask about research papers?

4385. What can I read about research papers?

4386. Who is in charge of the writing lab?

4387. How can I contact the writing lab?

4388. Where is the writing lab located?

4389. When is the writing lab open? Evenings? Weekends?

4390. What else should I know about writing research papers?

4391. How will my ability to write research papers affect my academic performance?

Presentations

4392. What experiences do students have preparing for and making presentations?

4393. What experiences do students have preparing for and giving speeches?

4394. What experiences do students have preparing for debates?

4395. Does the syllabus describe the requirements for oral presentations?

4396. How should I introduce my topic?

4397. How can I get the audience's attention?

4398. Should I provide evidence, supporting facts and examples during my presentation?

4399. How should I conclude and summarize my presentation?

4400. Should visual aids be used? Overheads? Slides? Handouts?

4401. Can I check out audio-visual equipment from the college?

4402. Can I check out a camera?

4403. How long can borrowed audio-visual equipment be kept?

4404. Where can I get help to make audio or video recordings, slides, charts, graphs, posters, or other graphics?

4405. Can I make arrangements to videotape my presentation?

4406. Should I practice the delivery of my presentation alone? In front of friends?

4407. What should I know about what my body language conveys to the audience?

4408. Should I make eye contact during my presentation?

4409. What if I have a fear of public speaking?

4410. Who can I ask about making presentations?

4411. What can I read about making presentations?

4412. What else should I know about making presentations?

4413. How will my ability to make presentations affect my academic performance?

Spiritual Experiences

4414. What experiences do students have with spirituality while in college?

4415. What should I know about values?

4416. What should I know about virtues?

4417. What should I know about vices?

4418. What should I know about morals?

4419. What should I know about ethics?

4420. What should I know about personal integrity?

4421. What should I know about religious life at this college?

4422. What should I know about meditation and prayer?

4423. What should I do if what is taught in class conflicts with my religious beliefs?

4424. Am I expected to participate in religious life and activities on campus?

4425. Is attendance at a religious service required at this college?

4426. Will this college notify appropriate campus organizations of my religious preference?

4427. Are there religious organizations on campus?

4428. Are there religious facilities on campus? Nearby?

4429. What time are religious services held? Which days?

4430. Who conducts religious services on campus?

4431. Are there opportunities to share my faith with other students on campus?

4432. Is there a campus ministry office on campus?

4433. Which denominations are represented in the on-campus ministry?

4434. What should I do if I am being pressured to join a religious group?

4435. What should I do if I am being pressured to make a financial contribution to a religious group?

4436. What should I do if a religious group suggests that I stop communicating with my friends or family?

4437. Who can I ask about my spirituality?

4438. What can I read about spirituality?

4439. Who is in charge of the campus ministry office?

4440. Where is the campus ministry office located?

4441. How can I contact the campus ministry office?

4442. When is the campus ministry office open? Evenings? Weekends?

4443. What else should I know about spiritual experiences at this college?

4444. How will my spirituality affect my academic performance?

FAQ's About Getting out of College

PART III

"Ask and it will be given to you; seek, and you will find; knock and it will be opened to you."

Matthew 7:7

Jigsaw puzzles were created as educational tools to help students learn and develop problem-solving skills. Each topic in this section provides you with an opportunity to step back and consider what you have accomplished thus far.

Consider what your graduation picture looks like? Ask if there are any holes in your job search? Are you ready to try to solve an even larger and more complex puzzle like graduate school? Take time to reflect on your entire college experience by asking how you have grown and developed over time, and whether you are better off as a result.

As a college graduate, think of yourself as a 'corner' piece. There may have been times during college when you felt backed into a corner. But corner pieces are the foundation for the frame of a puzzle. They have double the competitive edge.

Graduation Requirements

4445. How will I know I am eligible to graduate?

4446. What should I do in my last term?

4447. Must I meet with my advisor before graduation?

4448. Must I be registered for classes during the term I graduate?

4449. Is a portfolio required for graduation?

4450. Is a senior experience course required for graduation?

4451. Must I complete a graduation application?

4452. When is the deadline to apply for graduation?

4453. Under what circumstances will my graduation application be declined?

4454. Will my graduation application be approved if I have completed the correct number of credits?

4455. Will my graduation application be declined if I have completed the correct number of credits but haven't taken the right courses?

4456. Will my graduation application be declined if I have incomplete grades?

4457. Must I schedule an exit interview if I have received financial aid?

4458. Must I complete a graduating senior survey?

4459. Must I pass a state- or institutionally-mandated test to advance to the upper division?

4460. Must I pass a state- or institutionally-mandated test to graduate?

4461. What is the name of the required test?

4462. What does the test cover?

4463. What is a passing score on the test?

4464. How many opportunities will I have to pass the test?

4465. What happens if I don't pass the test?

4466. How will I be notified that my application has been approved?

4467. Who can I ask about graduation requirements?

4468. What can I read about graduation requirements?

4469. Who is in charge of graduation requirements?

4470. What else should I know about graduation requirements?

Job Searches

4471. What experiences do students at this college have finding work after graduation?

4472. How easy is it to find a job in my major?

4473. How many students in my major find employment immediately after graduation?

4474. Which local, state or national employers hire graduates in my major?

4475. What college resources are available to assist in my job search?

4476. How can potential employers be identified?

4477. How do I learn about job openings for graduates in my major?

4478. Where are job boards or lists of employment opportunities located?

4479. Which publications advertise for jobs in my field or major?

4480. How can I find appropriate Websites for my job search?

4481. Should I use an employment agency or a search firm to assist with my job search?

4482. What should I know about employment agencies?

4483. What should I know about agency and search firm fees?

4484. Should I ask for references from previous clients?

4485. How will I know which jobs I am qualified for?

4486. Who can help me complete an employment application?

4487. Who can help me prepare a resume?

4488. What are the different types of resume formats?

4489. What is a chronological resume format?

4490. What is a functional resume format?

4491. What is a combination resume format?

4492. Which format is preferred by employers in my major?

4493. How long is a typical resume?

4494. What information should be included in my resume?

4495. Which action verbs should be included in my resume?

4496. Which font and type size should be used in my resume?

4497. What type of paper should be used to print my resume?

4498. What is the purpose of a cover letter?

4499. What should be included in a cover letter?

4500. Should cover letters be personalized for each job?

4501. Should a resume be sent without a cover letter?

4502. Should my resume be faxed to an employer?

4503. Should my resume be posted on the Internet?

4504. Does this college provide placement services?

4505. Which academic degree programs utilize placement services the most?

4506. How can I register for placement services?

4507. How long will this college keep my credentials on file?

4508. What is informational interviewing?

4509. What should I know about the company I want to work for?

4510. Should I ask how long the company has been in business?

4511. Should I ask what the company makes, sells, serves or manufactures?

4512. Should I talk to other employees about the company?

4513. Should I ask what it is like to work at that company?

4514. Should I ask where the company is located?

4515. Should I ask what community life is like in that company's location?

4516. Will I work at the main office or a different location?

4517. What should I know about the position for which I am applying?

4518. Should I ask which tasks and activities will be performed on a daily basis?

4519. Should I ask who supervises the position?

4520. Should I ask if the position will be responsible for supervising others?

4521. Should I ask if the position requires managing a budget?

4522. Should I ask if there are opportunities for advancement?

4523. Who can I ask about job searches?

4524. What can I read about job searches?

4525. What else should I know about searching for a job?

Employment Interviews

4526. What experiences do students have interviewing for jobs?

4527. Do employers conduct on-campus interviews? Which ones?

4528. Where can I locate an on-campus interview schedule?

4529. Can arrangements be made for video or remote interviews?

4530. What do employers look for in a prospective employee?

4531. What is behavior-based interviewing?

4532. Should I be prepared to discuss my background and experience?

4533. Should I be prepared to discuss my strengths and weakness?

4534. Should I be prepared to explain why I think I am qualified for the position?

4535. Should I be prepared to discuss why I should be selected instead of another equally qualified candidate?

4536. Will I be asked where I would like to be in three to five years?

4537. Should I be prepared to explain gaps in my employment history?

4538. Should I be prepared to provide examples of how I have handled conflict in the workplace?

4539. Will I be asked to take and pass a drug test?

4540. Will I be asked to take and pass a psychological exam?

4541. Will I be asked to pass a criminal background check?

4542. Will my credit be checked?

4543. Will I need to provide proof of my degree or other credentials?

4544. How early should I arrive for my interview?

4545. What should I wear to the interview?

4546. What should I know about lunch or dinner interviews?

4547. What should I know about business etiquette?

4548. How do I handle questions about salary during an interview?

4549. What is the salary range for the position?

4550. What should I know about negotiating a salary?

4551. What should I know about negotiating fringe benefits?

4552. What should I know about signing an employment contract?

4553. Who can I ask about employment interviews?

4554. What can I read about employment interviews?

4555. Who is in charge of employment interviews?

4556. What else should I know about employment interviews?

Graduate School

4557. Should I continue my college education after receiving a bachelor's degree?

4558. Is a graduate degree required for advancement in my field or company?

4559. Should I consider graduate school if I am interested in conducting scholarly research?

4560. Should I consider graduate school simply because I don't know what to do after undergraduate school?

4561. Should I consider graduate school because I am unable to find a good job?

4562. What can I do with a graduate degree?

4563. Which professions require a graduate degree for employment?

4564. Which fields or jobs require education beyond the bachelor's degree?

4565. Must I take a licensure or certification exam to work in my major?

4566. Must I have a graduate degree to sit for an exam or apply for certification?

4567. How many students in my major enter graduate school immediately after graduation?

4568. Do I have to apply right away?

4569. How different is graduate school from undergraduate school?

4570. Is the graduate program I am interested in offered at several institutions?

4571. How do I decide which graduate school to attend?

4572. What distinguishes one graduate program from another?

4573. Is graduate school more specialized?

4574. Does graduate school require working more closely with faculty in my field?

4575. Are graduate classes smaller?

4576. Are academic standards higher in graduate school?

4577. Will I have to attend full time? Part time?

4578. Does graduate school require a high level of academic commitment?

4579. How does the undergraduate

admissions process differ from the graduate admissions process?

4580. Is getting into graduate school more competitive?

4581. Who makes graduate admissions decisions? Faculty committees? The dean? An administrator?

4582. What do graduate admissions committees look for in an applicant?

4583. Will the committee look at my potential to do scholarly research?

4584. Does the department prefer applicants immediately out of undergraduate programs?

4585. Does the department prefer applicants with work or research experience?

4586. How much work experience should I have before applying to graduate school?

4587. Before applying should I make sure someone on the graduate school faculty shares my research interests?

4588. How can I learn more about the backgrounds and interests of graduate school faculty?

4589. Should I identify graduate school faculty who are experts at what I want to learn?

4590. Should I read the books, journal articles and other works of graduate school faculty?

4591. Does the academic department I am interested in publish a journal?

4592. Should I determine which research areas I find most interesting?

4593. How can I determine who is doing the best research in my area of interest?

4594. Should I read extensively the literature from my field of interest?

4595. Should my interests and the interests of my graduate school faculty match?

4596. Should I try to arrange an interview with a graduate school faculty member?

4597. What is a statement of purpose or statement of intent?

4598. What will a graduate school admissions committee look for in my statement of purpose?

4599. How does a graduate school statement of purpose differ from an undergraduate application essay?

4600. Should my statement be tailored to the department to which I am applying?

4601. Should my statement of purpose address why I want to go to graduate school?

4602. Should my statement express an interest in research, teaching and publishing?

4603. Should my statement of purpose address which research topics, are of interest to me?

4604. If admitted, will I be required to conduct the kind of research discussed in my application?

4605. Will the admissions committee consider my recommendation letters?

4606. How do graduate recommendation letters differ from undergraduate school?

4607. How do recommendation letters for immediate graduates differ from graduates who apply with work or research experience?

4608. Should graduate school recommendation letters focus on why I belong in graduate school?

4609. Do recommendation letters from well-known faculty members carry more weight with the admissions committee?

4610. When are graduate school applications due? December? January?

4611. Is a supplemental application form required?

4612. Which graduate exams are required in general?

4613. Which graduate exams are required to apply to medical school?

4614. Which graduate exams are required to apply to business school?

4615. Which graduate exams are required to apply to law school?

4616. Which graduate exams are required to apply to dental school?

4617. Must transcripts be sent from all my undergraduate institutions?

4618. Must I provide proof of a required license or certification?

4619. What are the chances of being admitted to a graduate program at my undergraduate institution?

4620. Must my undergraduate institution verify that I was not subject to any disciplinary actions while enrolled there?

4621. Must a resume be submitted with my application?

4622. How will I pay for graduate studies?

4623. What is a fellowship?

4624. What is an assistantship?

4625. What is a tuition waiver?

4626. Are fellowships, assistantships or tuition waivers renewable?

4627. Are fellowships, assistantships or tuition waivers considered taxable income?

4628. Can I work while enrolled in the program?

4629. Should I have enough money to complete graduate school without having to work in an outside job?

4630. Will I have to use my personal savings?

4631. Will a family member or spouse need to subsidize me?

4632. Am I willing to borrow money to complete my graduate degree?

4633. How many years of study beyond the bachelor's degree are required to receive a master's degree?

4634. What are the course requirements for a master's degree in my area of interest?

4635. Will admission to a master's program automatically lead to a doctoral program?

4636. How many years of study beyond a master's degree are required to receive a specialist degree?

4637. How many years of study beyond a master's degree are required to receive a doctoral degree?

4638. Does the doctoral program confer a master's or specialist degree at the halfway point?

4639. What is a thesis?

4640. Are the requirements the same for a master's and doctoral thesis?

4641. What are the doctoral degree course requirements in my area of interest?

4642. Will pursuit of a doctorate require me to conduct original research?

4643. What is a dissertation?

4644. How do I select a suitable dissertation topic?

4645. Should I select a topic I will be interested over a long period of time?

4646. How do I generate a research question?

4647. Must I review the literature pertaining to my study?

4648. How will I know when I have read enough literature?

4649. How important is it to read original source documents?

4650. Should I rely on someone else's interpretation of the original source document?

4651. Must I identify the problem that my research may help solve or alleviate?

4652. Must I identify and form a faculty committee to supervise my research?

4653. How many people should be on my committee?

4654. What is the role of committee?

4655. Is the committee responsible for ensuring that my research meets college standards?

4656. Must I take qualifying or comprehensive exams?

4657. Must I write a research proposal?

4658. Must I describe the method of inquiry to be used to answer my research question?

4659. Must I describe how research data will be collected?

4660. Must I receive consent from all the people I will be studying?

4661. What ethical principles or codes are relevant to my field and my study?

4662. Must I describe how I will analyze the data?

4663. Will written guidelines be provided on how to submit my manuscript?

4664. Must I schedule an oral proposal or dissertation defense?

4665. How should I handle fears and doubts about my ability to complete a dissertation?

4666. Must an article be published before graduation?

4667. Should I become a member of a professional organization in my field?

4668. Can professional organizations be joined at reduced student rates?

4669. Must I present a paper at a major regional or national conference in my field?

4670. What is the time limit for completing the doctoral program?

4671. What happens if I exceed the time limit?

4672. Can the time limit be extended? Under what circumstances?

4673. Are deferments or extensions made for unanticipated and compelling reasons?

4674. When a deferment or extension is

granted, will my financial aid also be deferred?

4675. Should I continue my education beyond the doctorate?

4676. What is post-doctoral study?

4677. Do I need a sponsor for postdoctoral study?

4678. What common mistakes do graduate applicants make?

4679. How can I contact the graduate studies office?

4680. Where is the graduate studies office located?

4681. When is the graduate studies office open? Evenings? Weekends?

4682. Do I need an appointment to meet with graduate studies staff?

4683. Are fees charged for services provided to graduate students?

4684. Who can I ask about graduate school?

4685. What can I read about graduate school?

4686. Who is in charge of graduate admissions?

4687. How can I contact the graduate admissions office?

4688. Where is the graduate admissions office located?

4689. When is the graduate admissions office open? Evenings? Weekends?

4690. What else should I know about graduate school?

Commencement

4691. How will I know if I am eligible to participate in commencement?

4692. Will I receive information about commencement activities? When? How?

4693. What must I do to participate in commencement exercises?

4694. What are Latin honors?

4695. How will I be notified if I am graduating *cum laude*?

4696. How will I be notified if I am graduating *magna cum laude*?

4697. How will I be notified if I am graduating *summa cum laude*?

4698. Are there other opportunities for me to graduate with distinction?

4699. How many graduation ceremonies are held in an academic year? When?

4700. Can I participate in commencement if I only have one term left before finishing my degree?

4701. How many people can be invited to commencement?

4702. Are tickets required?

4703. How many tickets will I receive?

4704. What should I wear to commencement?

4705. Must I wear a traditional cap, gown and/or hood?

4706. Must these items be purchased? Can I rent it? Borrow it?

4707. When is the deadline to order a cap, gown and hood?

4708. For the bachelor's degrees, is the tassel worn on the right at the beginning of the ceremony and moved to the left at the conclusion of the ceremony?

4709. For graduate degrees is the tassel worn on the left throughout the ceremony?

4710. What color tassel, hood and trim is associated with different academic disciplines?

4711. Is maize the color for agriculture?

4712. Is white the color for arts, letters and humanities?

4713. Is drab the color for business?

4714. Is lilac the color for dentistry?

4715. Is copper the color for economics?

4716. Is light blue the color for education?

4717. Is orange the color for engineering?

4718. Is brown the color for fine arts and architecture?

4719. Is russet the color for forestry?

4720. Is crimson the color for journalism?

4721. Is purple the color for law?

4722. Is lemon the color for library science?

4723. Is green the color for medicine?

4724. Is pink the color for music?

4725. Is apricot the color for nursing?

4726. Is silver gray the color for speech and oratory?

4727. Is olive green the color for pharmacy?

4728. Is dark blue the color for philosophy?

4729. Is sage green the color for physical education?

4730. Is peacock the color for public administration?

4731. Is blue the color for foreign service?

4732. Is salmon pink the color for public health?

4733. Is golden yellow the color for science?

4734. Is citron the color for social work?

4735. Is scarlet the color for theology?

4736. Is gray the color for veterinary science?

4737. What are the differences between caps, gowns, hoods and sleeves for associate, bachelor's, master's, specialist, and doctoral degrees?

4738. What happens at a commencement ceremony?

4739. What is the preliminary processional?

4740. Who are members of the platform party?

4741. Who leads the processional? A mace bearer? A chief marshall?

4742. Is there a commencement speaker?

4743. Who is the speaker?

4744. How are speakers selected?

4745. Can I suggest a commencement speaker?

4746. When are earned degrees conferred?

4747. When are honorary degrees conferred?

4748. What is the subsequent processional?

4749. How long does the commencement ceremony last?

4750. Where can I get a copy of the commencement program?

4751. Will my name appear in the commencement program?

4752. Will there be an official photographer at the commencement ceremony?

4753. Will I receive my degree at commencement?

4754. Can I request a second copy of my degree?

4755. How do I purchase a college ring?

4756. How long will it take to receive a ring?

4757. Who can I ask about commencement?

4758. What can I read about commencement?

4759. Who is in charge of commencement?

4760. How can I contact the commencement office?

4761. Where is the commencement office located?

4762. When is the commencement office open? Evenings? Weekends?

4763. What else should I know about commencement?

Alumni Associations

4764. What experiences do graduates have in the alumni association?

4765. What are the benefits of alumni association membership?

4766. As an alumnus, what college services are available to me?

4767. Does alumni membership include access to an alumni house?

4768. Does alumni membership include access to the library?

4769. Does alumni membership include access to the career center?

4770. Does alumni membership include access to the computer center?

4771. As an alumnus, will I have an e-mail account?

4772. Will I receive an alumni magazine?

4773. How is news submitted to the alumni magazine?

4774. Will the alumni association help locate my former classmates?

4775. Will I receive invitations to alumni events?

4776. Which types of alumni events are planned? Homecoming? Group travel? Lectures?

4777. Will I have an opportunity to serve on planning committees?

4778. How can I join the alumni association?

4779. How much are membership fees?

4780. Will I receive a membership card?

4781. How are alumni association officers selected or elected?

4782. Do members of the alumni body have voting privileges?

4783. Is there a regional alumni association in my hometown?

4784. Who are some of this college's most famous alumni?

4785. What is the alumni giving rate at this college?

4786. How can I make a gift or pledge to this college?

4787. What are the different ways to make a gift?

4788. What types of assets can be used to make a gift?

4789. What is a matching gift?

4790. What is an endowed gift?

4791. What is a bequest to the college?

4792. Can my gift be designated for a specific or special purpose?

4793. Can my gift be made online?

4794. How will my gift be recognized?

4795. What tax deduction will I receive for my gift?

4796. Who can I ask about the alumni association?

4797. What can I read about the alumni association?

4798. Who is in charge of the alumni association?

4799. How can I contact the alumni association?

4800. Where is the alumni association office located?

4801. When is the alumni association office open? Evenings? Weekends?

4802. What else should I know about alumni affairs?

College Outcomes

Personal Outcomes

4803. How will I personally grow, develop or change in college?

4804. Will I have a clearer picture or vision of what my future life will be like?

4805. Will I have a better understanding of my desired role in society?

4806. Will I be able to identify what motivates me internally?

4807. Will I be able to identify what motivates me externally?

4808. Will I be able to evaluate my strengths and weaknesses realistically?

4809. Will I have a better understanding of who I am?

4810. Will I develop my own identity?

4811. Will I become more independent?

4812. Will I be able to practice good health and fitness habits?

4813. Will I be able to lead a balanced life?

4814. Will I be able to manage my emotions?

4815. Will I know how to handle stress and anxiety?

4816. Will I know how to maintain my composure in stressful situations?

4817. Will I be more mature?

4818. Will I be more flexible and adaptable?

4819. Will I be able to formulate realistic, measurable and attainable goals?

4820. Will I be able to develop an action plan to achieve my goals?

4821. Will I know what to do on a daily basis to achieve my goals?

4822. Will I be able to mobilize myself into action?

4823. Will I be able to manage my time effectively?

4824. Will I be able to stay focused on my goals and avoid distractions?

4825. Will I know the location or environment I need to be in to achieve my goals?

4826. Will I know which human and material resources are needed to achieve my goals?

4827. Will I know how to ask for and receive help?

4828. Will I be able to define obstacles and problems that impede my progress?

4829. Will I be able to generate solutions or alternative approaches?

4830. Will I be able to weigh the advantages and disadvantages of each solution?

4831. Will I be able to consider alternatives until a solution is found?

4832. Will I be able to examine and take responsibility for my behavior?

4833. Will I be able to accept the consequences of my actions?

4834. Who can I ask about personal outcomes?

4835. What can I read about personal outcomes?

4836. What else should I know about personal outcomes?

Interpersonal Outcomes

4837. How will my relationships with others form, develop or change in college?

4838. Will I have a clearer picture of what my future relationships with others will be like?

4839. Will I be able to identify what motivates me to start, remain in or leave a relationship?

4840. Will I be able to cultivate and develop close friendships?

4841. Will I be able to develop a network or support group?

4842. Will I be able to make good first impressions on others?

4843. Will I have knowledge of and be able to use good manners?

4844. Will I be open to the ideas and processes of others?

4845. Will I be able to see multiple sides of issues?

4846. Will I be able to give and receive compliments?

4847. Will I be able to give and receive constructive criticism?

4848. Will I be able to respond appropriately to constructive criticism?

4849. Will I be able to recognize and acknowledge authority figures?

4850. Will I be able to function as a member of a team?

4851. Will I be able to cooperate with others to accomplish a common goal?

4852. Will I be able to influence or persuade others to act?

4853. Will I be able to help others achieve their desired results?

4854. Will I be able to get along with others?

4855. Will I be able to get along with people who have different personality types?

4856. Will I be able to get along with people who have different perspectives?

4857. Will I have knowledge of sex roles and gender differences?

4858. Will I have knowledge of people from different races and religions?

4859. Will I be able to recognize cultural variations in communication?

4860. Will I be able to express empathy and sympathy toward others?

4861. Will I be able to express compassion toward others?

4862. Will I be able to help others who are in difficulty?

4863. Will I be able to trust others?

4864. Will I be able to make and keep promises and commitments to others?

4865. Will I be able to apologize to and forgive others?

4866. Will I be able to discern the positive and negative affects I have on other people?

4867. Will I have knowledge of when to be passive, assertive and aggressive with others?

4868. Will I have knowledge of how intimidation, sarcasm, tactlessness, arrogance, domination, and self-centeredness affect others?

4869. Will I know how to resolve conflicts diplomatically?

4870. Will I be able to respect the property of others?

4871. Who can I ask about interpersonal outcomes?

4872. What can I read about interpersonal outcomes?

4873. What else should I know about interpersonal outcomes?

Career Outcomes

4874. How will my career aspirations form, develop or change in college?

4875. Will I have a clearer picture of what my future career path will look like?

4876. Will I be able to identify what motivates me to pursue, remain in or leave a job?

4877. Will I be able to use my knowledge, skills and abilities to meet the needs of others?

4878. Will I have a better chance of being hired for a job?

4879. Will I be more likely to have improved job fit?

4880. Will I be more likely to have increased job satisfaction?

4881. Will I have the potential to become an authority in my field?

4882. Will I have the potential to be recognized by colleagues for contributions to my field?

4883. Will I have knowledge of the vision, motivation, strategies, goals and culture of the organization for whom I work?

4884. Will I be able to articulate an organizational vision?

4885. Will I have knowledge of organizational structure?

4886. Will I have knowledge of the laws, policies, and procedures impacting my organization?

4887. Will I be able to perform the work specified in my job description?

4888. Will I be able to work independently?

4889. Will I be able to take direction?

4890. Will I have knowledge of how my work affects the work of others?

4891. Will I have a better chance of being promoted?

4892. Will I be able to recruit, interview, hire and retain employees?

4893. Will I be able to manage a budget and allocate resources?

4894. Will I be able to manage a project from start to finish?

4895. Will I have organizational responsibility for the work of others?

4896. Will I be able to evaluate the work and performance of others?

4897. Will I be able to teach new skills to others?

4898. Will I be able to take charge of a situation when necessary and appropriate?

4899. Will I be able to become successful in my own business?

4900. Will I be able to cultivate relationships with customers, clients, and suppliers?

4901. Will I be able to negotiate mutually beneficial outcomes?

4902. Who can I ask about career outcomes?

4903. What can I read about career outcomes?

4904. What else should I know about career outcomes?

Financial Outcomes

4905. How will my personal finances form, develop or change in college?

4906. Will I have a clearer picture of what my future potential earnings will look like?

4907. Will I be able to identify what motivates me to pursue, maintain or relinquish financial security?

4908. Will I be better off financially?

4909. Will I have increased social mobility?

4910. Will my socioeconomic status be improved?

4911. Will I be able to make charitable contributions?

4912. Will the quality of life for my spouse and children be improved?

4913. Will the quality of my leisure time be improved?

4914. Will I be knowledgeable of consumer behavior?

4915. Will I be knowledgeable of how my decisions affect my financial circumstances?

4916. Will I be able to weigh the costs of something against the benefits?

4917. Will I be credit worthy?

4918. Who can I ask about financial outcomes?

4919. What can I read about financial outcomes?

4920. What else should I know about financial outcomes?

Environmental Outcomes

4921. How will my role in the community form, develop or change in college?

4922. Will I have a clearer picture of what my geographic area and community will look like in the future?

4923. Will I be able to identify what motivates me to select, live in and remain in a geographic area or community?

4924. Will I develop a social conscience?

4925. Will I have improved social status in the community?

4926. Will I have knowledge of my community's governance structure?

4927. Will I be able to use my community's resources?

4928. Will I be able to volunteer for a social cause?

4929. Will I be able to address social problems in the community?

4930. Will I be able to participate in community activities?

4931. Will I be able to influence the political structure of my community?

4932. Will I be able to become a community leader?

4933. Will I be able to form social and political values?

4934. Will I be able to exercise my civil rights and liberties?

4935. Will I be able to protect the natural and manmade resources of my community?

4936. Will I have knowledge of the problems facing my nation, state and community?

4937. Will I have knowledge of global issues?

4938. Who can I ask about environmental outcomes?

4939. What can I read about environmental outcomes?

4940. What else should I know about environmental outcomes?

Educational Outcomes

4941. How will my knowledge form, develop or change in college?

4942. Will I have a clearer picture of what I know at present and what I need to learn in the future?

4943. Will I be able to identify what motivates me to pursue, persist or abandon higher education?

4944. Will I have the desire to pursue life-long learning?

4945. Will I have increased educational attainment?

4946. Will I develop intellectual self-confidence?

4947. Will I have knowledge of a particular field or discipline?

4948. Will I have subject matter competence in my major field?

4949. Will I be able to seek, record, study, recall, transmit and apply information?

4950. Will I be able to comprehend, apply, analyze, synthesize and evaluate information?

4951. Will I be able to think logically without being influenced by personal bias?

4952. Will I have knowledge of the importance of history as it relates to the past and informs the present?

4953. Will I have knowledge of different philosophies, cultures and ways of life?

4954. Will I be able to demonstrate mathematical ability?

4955. Will I be able to analyze data using statistics?

4956. Will I be able to analyze quantitative problems?

4957. Will I have knowledge of new developments in science and technology?

4958. Will I be able to demonstrate computer literacy

4959. Will I be able to prepare and produce different types of written material?

4960. Will I be able to proof-read and edit the work of others?

4961. Will I have knowledge of acceptable rules of language and grammar?

4962. Will I be able to demonstrate observation skills?

4963. Will I be able to ask questions to gather information and clarify meaning?

4964. Will I be able to listen attentively?

4965. Will I be able to avoid interrupting?

4966. Will I be able to send and receive effective verbal, non-verbal and written messages?

4967. Will I be aware of non-verbal communication such as gestures, body language and facial expressions?

4968. Will I be able to communicate the opinions, observations and conclusion of others accurately?

4969. Will I be able to speak and express myself in public?

4970. Will I be able to deliver effective oral presentations?

4971. Will I be able to send messages that are appropriate for the audience and accomplishes their intended purpose?

4972. Will I be able to adjust or adapt my speaking manner and style to the audience and situation?

4973. Will I be able to provide appropriate supporting evidence when communicating?

4974. Will I be able to have conversations about current events?

4975. Will I be able to have conversations about social issues?

4976. Will I be able to have conversations about literature?

4977. Will I be able to have conversations about the arts?

4978. Will I be able to have conversations about scientific theories?

4979. Will I be able to have conversations about the economy?

4980. Will I be able to have conversations about international relations?

4981. Will I be able to pursue further education in a professional, scientific or scholarly field?

4982. Who can I ask about educational outcomes?

4983. What can I read about educational outcomes?

4984. What else should I know about educational outcomes?

Spiritual Outcomes

4985. How will my spirituality form, develop or change when I am in college?

4986. Will I have a clearer picture of what I want my future spiritual life to look like?

4987. Will I be able to identify what motivates me to seek, practice or abandon spirituality in my life?

4988. Will I have knowledge of my purpose in life?

4989. Will I have knowledge of what influences me?

4990. Will I develop spiritual values?

4991. Will I be able to set spiritual goals?

4992. Will I develop morally?

4993. Will I develop ethically?

4994. Will I be able to formulate a spiritual philosophy?

4995. Will I be able to develop a set of standards or code of conduct that governs and regulates my life?

4996. Will I be able to act with integrity?

4997. Will I be able to integrate spirituality into my life?

4998. Will I be able to model, demonstrate and personify the beliefs and convictions that govern my life?

4999. Will I formulate religious values?

5000. Will I be able to develop a religious identification?

5001. Will I be able to apply and practice religious principles in my life?

5002. Will I be able to follow a pre-set order or worship?

5003. Will I become involved in a worshipping community?

5004. Will I become active in a religious organization?

5005. Who can I ask about spiritual outcomes?

5006. What can I read about spiritual outcomes?

5007. What else should I know about spiritual outcomes?

Overwhelmed?

Enroll in the College Life Skills Course®

The College Life Skills Course® is an early, comprehensive, enlightening and rigorous introduction to a life management system that asks seven major questions that *college bound* students must answer to become *college graduates*.

To download or request a brochure and current schedule of courses, visit us online at:

www.collegelifeskills.com.

ABOUT THE AUTHOR

Dr. Rozalia Williams, Founder and President of Hidden Curriculum Education, Inc. developed the A7MQ™ life management system taught in the two-day intensive College Life Skills Course®. A college administrator for over twenty years, she has devoted her professional career to creating, implementing and evaluating student development programs. She has over 20 years of experience providing sound advice to high school, undergraduate and graduate students while serving in numerous executive, administrative and instructional positions at public and private universities in Florida. She earned a Bachelor's in Journalism and a Master's in Counselor Education from Florida International University; and a Doctor of Education degree in Administration, Planning and Social Policy from Harvard University. Her experiences as a sixteen-year-old college student, retention counselor, pre-college program director, assistant to the vice president of student affairs, branch campus director, assistant dean and instructor of first year experience courses at two- and four-year institutions frame the questions for this book.

Question Index